Buying Time ~ Storing Memories

Buying Time ~ Storing Memories

᚛᚜

CAROLE BROWNING - BLACK

This book was printed in the United States of America.

To order additional copies of this book, contact:
Xlibris Corporation
1-888-795-4274
www.Xlibris.com
Orders@Xlibris.com
107035

In loving memory of our Special Angel

DISCLAIMER

This book is a memoir written from the perspective and the memory of the mother. Names were changed when it was necessary to protect the privacy of the people involved.

Time is really the only capital
That any human being has,
And the one thing that he
Can't afford to lose.

Thomas Alva Edison

August 11, 1991

The heat radiating from the stone breezeway coupled with the water cascading from the hose formed mini rainbows in the blazing sun. The steam rising from the stone fogged my glasses, but the occasional droplet of water that landed and then splashed onto my legs was a welcome relief from the oppressive heat. The hot, sultry dog days of August were here. If we weren't breaking any records today, we were very close, and the humidity made it seem even hotter. The pool would be a popular place this afternoon.

Dragging the hose over to the other end of the breezeway, I sprayed the cement walkway that circled the pool, emptied the skimmer basket, and threw the inner tube and diving sticks into the deep end.

Just as I started to wind up the hose, next to the back door, I heard a loud thump. Startled, I looked over my shoulder. Nothing there. Then I heard a bumping sound. It was coming from inside the house. Stephanie. She'd been sitting at the dining room table coloring in her picture book.

Dropping the hose and darting up the steps to the back door, I rushed through the kitchen, visually searching the dining room. "Oh, my God," I cried. Stephanie's thin, frail body was lying on the floor contorting, her arms and legs were thrashing, and her head was pounding against a chair. A deep guttural sound emanated from her throat.

"Stephanie. Stephanie." My voice trembled as I called her name. I tried to cradle her body in my arms. Seizure. She was having a seizure. I had seen children in the throes of a seizure before. What do I do? I couldn't think. My mind was frozen.

Calm down, I told myself. You have to take charge. No one else is around. A spoon. A spoon. Something to put in her mouth. I'd heard that people having seizures could bite off their tongue or even swallow it.

Before I could get to the cupboard and find a spoon, her body relaxed and her arms and legs became limp. Folding her into my arms, I rocked her back and forth, moaning her name. "Stephanie, Stephanie. Can you hear Mommy talking to you? Are you okay? Can you see me, honey? It's Mommy." Tears ran down my face.

Her body tensed and the contortions began again. Forgetting about the spoon, I released her, and rushed to the telephone. Dialing 911, I begged them to answer. At the sound of a voice, I shouted, "I need an ambulance! I don't know what's happening to my daughter! She's on the floor, and I think she's having a seizure. Hurry!"

"Okay, Ma'am, can you tell me where you live?"

"I live . . . I live . . ." Again my mind was frozen.

"Calm down, Ma'am," the operator instructed, "and just tell me the street name and number. I know the town you're calling from."

In a surge of memory, the number and name of the street came into my head. Blurting it into the mouthpiece, I slammed the phone down and rushed back to hold Stephanie close. Blood was trickling from the corner of her mouth. She had bitten her tongue, but, once again, her body had relaxed and her limbs were still.

By the time the ambulance and the EMTs arrived, Stephanie was alert and crying. "Mommy, my tongue's sore, and it tastes funny in my mouth. Ooh, my head hurts." Her eyes darted from one stranger to the other. "I'm so tired, Mommy," she sighed, her head rolling to one side.

"It's okay, sweetheart. You'll be fine." Shoving the chairs away from the dining room table, I struggled to make more working room for the EMTs. "You just had an accident and fell off the chair." Trying to stay out of the way, but wanting to be close enough to touch and reassure her, I crawled underneath the table, stretched my hand out, and rubbed her arm.

They examined her thoroughly. Finding only bumps and bruises from the fall and the thrashing about, the chief technician suggested that they could take Stephanie to the hospital, or we could contact our family doctor and have him evaluate her. "Just remember," he said, standing over Stephanie and studying her face, "people don't have seizures for no reason."

"What's going on? What happened?" Ronnie rushed through the back door, his face pale, his eyes crinkled in concern. Tiny beads of perspiration formed on his forehead and trickled down the sides of his face.

Scrambling from beneath the table and struggling to my feet, I babbled, "We're okay. Stephanie had a couple seizures, but she's fine now. At least I think she's fine. She's fine right?" I smiled faintly and turned my head towards where Stephanie was lying and the EMTs were packing up their equipment.

"Hey, Babe, it's okay. Daddy's here now." He knelt beside her, picked her up, held her against his shoulder, and carried her into the living room.

As the ambulance crew pulled away from the house, I collapsed on the living room sofa, next to Stephanie, tears streaming down my face. "It's okay Mommy," Stephanie said, stroking my arm. "Why are you crying?"

She pulled herself up onto my lap, leaned over, and put her face against mine. How ironic, I thought. Stephanie, who all her life has faced one obstacle after another, was soothing me. I gathered her into my arms and rocked her gently. Why was I crying? The chief's words rang in my ears. *'People don't have seizures for no reason.'*

Could her condition be the reason for the seizures, I wondered? It wasn't likely, I reasoned. Never had any of her many doctors indicated that her mental retardation and her physical handicaps could result in seizures. Stephanie was twenty-five years old now, and her many problems had been identified and dealt with many years ago.

Because of her short stature and immaturely developed body, standing a little over four feet tall and weighing just sixty-five pounds, people found it hard to believe that she was as old as she was. Most people assumed that she was seven or eight, so her appearance was an advantage for her. No one expected too much from her. No one expected her to act like a twenty-five year old young woman.

Her underdeveloped body was an advantage for me too. I had less explaining to do. At least at first. Of course, after people were around Stephanie for a while, they realized that she had comprehension and mobility problems, and had a subtle, but noticeable shaking of her head. Then the questions would start.

Never having felt ashamed of her or the problems that she had, I resented their reactions when they learned that she was an adult who operated on the level of a five or six year old child. "Oh, I'm so sorry," they would say, looking embarrassed and sad at the same time, the pity showing plainly on their faces.

I didn't want their sympathy.

When did she stop growing? I couldn't remember. I hadn't really noticed. She was within the normal range for height and weight for the first few years of her life, but some time after the routine doctor visits for the required shots, where they measured and weighed her regularly, her growth had slowed and eventually stopped. It had been so gradual, and we were so engrossed in her mental and motor skills deficiencies, that her lack of growth caught us by surprise.

Why did she stop growing? We didn't know why. Stephanie never fit into any of the mental retardation categories that were recognized by the medical community in the 1970s, so the doctors, after extensive examinations and rigorous testing, didn't know why she developed as she did. They simply classified her as *a freak of nature*.

Despite her lack of physical development, when she turned thirteen, she started her menstrual cycle. Though I often wondered what I would say and do if, and when, she did start, I was caught off guard the day that it happened.

"Mommy, I think I cut myself. I'm bleeding." Stephanie came into the bathroom dressed in her pajamas, ready to go to bed.

"Where?" I didn't see any blood on her hands, so I pushed up the sleeves of her pajama top.

"Down here Mommy." She scrunched up her face and looked down below her stomach.

Oh no. It was time to come up with an explanation.

We went into her bedroom and sat on the bed. How could I make her understand what was happening to her body?

I didn't want to scare her, and yet, I wanted to impress upon her that it wasn't something that she discussed with anyone other than me, her sisters, and, if necessary, her female teachers.

She wouldn't understand *the birds and the bee's* story, but I wanted her to know it would happen every month, she needed to know how to take care of herself, and that, at times, it could be painful. I told her it was our secret because it didn't happen to boys.

She listened intently. When I was finished, she crossed her arms over her chest and said, "Hmm. I don't like this. Let's give it to the boys."

So, every month, thereafter, she would come and whisper in my ear that she had *started* and then she'd add, "C'mon, Mommy, let's give it to the boys." I'd smile and tell her that if there was any way to do it, I surely would.

Selfishly, I didn't mind that Stephanie was so petite for her age. It made it easier to cuddle with her. Any time, any place, she would slide onto my lap, nestle her head against my shoulder, her thick brown hair tickling my nose, wrap her skinny arms around my neck, look at me with her deep blue eyes, and whisper, "I love you, Mommy."

Feeling stronger and no longer frightened, Stephanie had disappeared upstairs to her bedroom. I tapped softly on her door and walked in. As usual, she was sitting with her back to the doorway, sprawled on the floor beside her bed, her legs bent at the knees, and her feet sticking out behind her. The music was blaring, much too loud, and she was singing along with Kenny Rogers to *Lucille*. Making a mental note to check the batteries in her hearing aids, I stood watching her.

Curious George was cradled in her left arm, and she was rocking him back and forth. Her right hand moved to her face, nudging her glasses up on her nose. The music stopped and she placed her right elbow on the small toy chest that stood against the wall beneath her window. Using it for leverage, she raised herself to a standing position. For a few seconds she wobbled like a gangly colt gaining its balance and then carried George to his bassinet.

"Now George," she said, as she spread a Mickey Mouse sheet over him, "if we go anywhere today, I'll take you with me." Straightening the sheet, she tucked it under his chin and then stuck his finger in his mouth. "But right now you hafta take a nap." She ran her hand down his cheek and leaned in and kissed him on the forehead. "And while you're takin' your nap, I'll clean up this mess you made on the floor." She sighed and shook her finger at him. "When you finish playin', you need to pick up your stuff and put it where it belongs." She gathered his plastic milk bottle, lettered blocks, and rubber farm animals, then lifted the lid of the toy chest and stuffed them all inside.

My heart ached for her. She and George were going some place today, but not where she might want to go.

"But I feel okay. I don't wanna go to the hospital." Stephanie stomped her foot as we walked into the living room.

"Sweetheart, Mommy and Daddy just want to make sure that there's nothing wrong so you don't fall off the chair again." I continued the lie that I had started earlier in the day.

Grasping her under her arms, I snatched her up and twirled her around the room. "Whee, let's dance and sing." I spun her around and around, singing, *"You are my Sunshine, My only Sunshine, You make me happy, When skies are gray . . . "* Gradually, her resistant and rigid body relaxed, and she sang along with me.

With one last spin, I toppled over onto the sofa, cradling her head against my neck, and whispered in her ear, "I love you more than you love me."

Recognizing one of the many *love games* that we played, she giggled and said, "No, I love you more that you love me." Worming her way out of my arms, she grasped my face between her tiny hands and started kissing me from my forehead to my chin.

"No," I protested, "I love you more than you love me."

Pushing me onto my back, she straddled my body, sitting on my stomach. "No, I love you more than you love me."

Knowing that, if allowed, she would make the game could go on and on, I worked my way into a sitting position. "You know what? We'll take you to the same hospital that Gramma's in so you'll get to see her." We would have gone to see her grandmother anyway, but mentioning her name always got positive results. "Won't that be fun?"

She smiled. "I'll get George." Next to George, Gramma was the one person that she enjoyed spending time with the most.

I didn't want to go to the hospital either, but if the seizures weren't part of Stephanie's condition, then what was causing them? And, if the seizures were a direct result of Stephanie's retardation, what was happening in her brain to cause this activity *now*, after all these years?

I wasn't sure I wanted to know.

From the day that Stephanie was born, there were little physical hints and clues that raised red flags in my mind. She slept too much. I understood that babies slept a lot; I already had one little girl, but Robyn had awakened often and demanded food and attention. Stephanie didn't. If I didn't wake her and feed her, she would sleep on contentedly. She showed no signs of hunger or discomfort from wet or dirty diapers.

So I tried to stimulate her. I held her, cuddled with her, rocked her, sang to her, read to her, stroked her face and nuzzled her neck. She appeared to enjoy the attention, but she never seemed to require it.

One day, while bathing her, I noticed an indentation at the base of her skull on one side of her head. "Ronnie," I called, "Come look at this." I felt a strange uneasiness, but Ronnie didn't think it was serious, and after a brief inspection, returned to his newspaper.

Though it made me feel better that he wasn't concerned, I still couldn't shake the nagging thoughts that cluttered my mind. If Stephanie was more alert and responsive, would I have ever given the small indentation a second thought? And since Stephanie wasn't as alert and responsive as Robyn was at her age, and since Robyn didn't have a noticeable indentation at the base of her skull, were the two conditions tied together and should I be concerned?

As these thoughts bounced around in my mind, I began to wonder, am I the quintessential mother who compares everything about her second child to everything about her first? Maybe, but at her next scheduled checkup, I would point out the indentation to Dr. Hampton.

Several weeks later, as I watched Dr. Hampton scrutinize the back of Stephanie's head, I anxiously held my breath and sought to convince myself that the indentation didn't mean anything. I watched his face for signs of concern.

He leaned his tall, slim frame over the examination table that stood opposite his cluttered desk. As he strained to get a closer look, his thick, dark glasses slid down his long, thin nose. After a few seconds, he raised his head, nodded, and grinned. "It's a good thing she's a girl. Her long hair will cover it up and no one will ever know it's there but you and Stephanie."

I allowed my breath to escape slowly. Good, I thought, and again, I felt better.

But, driving home, I struggled to reassure myself that Dr. Hampton was right. In spite of my desire to shove my fears aside, I couldn't rid myself of the one nagging fear that continued to invade my thoughts. Maybe I should be *more* worried about her unusual contentment than about the small indentation at the base of her skull. I looked at Stephanie in her carrier, sitting on the front seat. She wasn't fidgeting. She wasn't fussing. She wasn't sleeping. She was just staring straight ahead. A cold chill ran through my body.

As the weeks hurried on, I managed to push most of my worry to the back of my mind. But, one morning, as I put lotion on Stephanie's face, I looked long and hard at her eyes. They were not even. It wasn't real obvious, but one eye was slightly lower than the other one. I wouldn't mention it to anyone but Dr. Hampton, for if my fears were unfounded, there was no use projecting them onto other people. It was probably nothing.

As I sat in the waiting room, I wondered what Dr. Hampton's reaction would be this time. Maybe he'd tell me I should be glad that her eyes were slightly uneven instead of her nose being as big as mine or her ears as big as her father's. I needed to think funny thoughts to relieve the nervous tension building inside me. It was getting harder to clear my mind of the anxiety that never quite left.

Again, I watched Dr. Hampton's face for clues of concern while he inspected Stephanie's face. "Well, I can see that her eyes are not exactly even, but unless you pointed it out, I don't think I would have ever noticed it."

He leaned against the examination table, removed his thick, dark glasses and sighed. Was he getting exasperated by my picking out every little flaw in Stephanie's make-up?

"The truth is no one's eyes are exactly symmetrical." He took a step in my direction and leaned towards me, like he was studying the placement of my eyes. "The only person, besides you, who will ever notice that they're slightly uneven, is her boyfriend when he looks into her eyes and whispers sweet nothings."

But, again, on the drive home, nothing that I said to myself could shake the disconcerting thoughts that crept through my mind.

In the rush and distractions of everyday life, my worries over Stephanie got shoved to the back of my mind, again. Ronnie was back to teaching at the high school, Robyn was attending pre-kindergarten classes, and I was beginning preparations for the Christmas holidays.

And Stephanie was showing *some* progress. She was smiling, laughing, clapping and waving her hands. She was interacting with us.

Still she didn't seem to need or demand the attention that I associated with an infant. Still she slept too much.

On Christmas morning, Robyn's excitement was contagious, and although at five months of age, Stephanie didn't understand what was going on, she joined in by clapping her hands and giggling. She waved her arms and stretched to reach the ornaments and lights on the tree, but she didn't pay any attention to the gifts piled around it.

Robyn had graduated from being a cowgirl to being Boy, the son of Tarzan. Each week we would watch Tarzan, starring Ron Ely, as Robyn huddled in front of the television set straining to see every bit of action.

When the program was finished, Robyn would disappear behind the sofa and reappear in nothing but her underpants. Whooping and hollering, she would swing from imaginary grape vines, throw imaginary spears, and wrestle with imaginary jungle beasts.

Now her spears and animals wouldn't have to be imaginary. "Wow! Mommy, look at this spear." Robyn tore through the paper and ripped open the box. "Mommy, Daddy, look! Santa Claus brought me all kinds of animals." She shredded another box. In her excitement, she scattered animals, rubber spears, and numerous other goodies all around the room.

Scampering behind the sofa, she removed her pajamas and dashed out in her underpants waving a spear and grunting as she chased her father around the living room. "I'm Boy," she said, in her most authoritative voice. "I help Tarzan. I hunt wild animals. I live in the jungle."

Ronnie ran around the living room, trying to avoid being speared. "Don't hurt me Boy. I'll get out of your jungle," he shouted.

Robyn, in the excitement of chasing her father, forgot her role and began giggling and prancing around the room. He swept her up in his arms and tickled her squirming body, the spears and animals abandoned.

Stephanie sat on my lap contentedly absorbing the commotion. I put her on the floor, next to her pile of gifts, and propped her up with pillows, but she just sat complacently. I had hoped that she would attempt to grab her toys, rip some paper off of a box, roll over and start crawling towards the tree, reach out to take part in the hubbub that surrounded her. Anything.

Next year, I told myself. Next year Stephanie will be running around pretending to be someone or something. She won't be content to sit on my lap and watch.

I wasn't sure I believed it, but I wanted to.

As we began our post-holiday routine, I had more time to dwell on the little things that I had noticed about Stephanie, little things that I had shelved during the Christmas rush.

I stood in the doorway to the family room clutching Robyn's baby book to my chest. Ronnie was sitting in his reclining chair, across from the TV, working his crossword puzzle. "Can you remember how old Robyn was when she started sitting up by herself?" I asked the question with foreboding. There's something about verbalizing your fears that makes them more real. I wanted his input, but I was afraid of what I knew I would hear.

He looked up from his puzzle and rubbed the whiskers on his chin. The small furrows in his forehead told me he was thinking.

"Wasn't she sitting up by the time she was six months old?" His reply was nonchalant and unconcerned, but his words only reinforced my fears.

I *knew* Robyn had been sitting up by herself by six months; I had recorded it in her baby book, but I had hoped his memory would show that I had somehow made a mistake when recording the event.

No mistake. I knew this. I was clutching at straws.

I spent an afternoon at the library reading books and magazine articles about early childhood development, and the doctors agreed that it was normal for a baby to be sitting without support by six months. Stephanie sat in her carrier and looked around at the many rows of books as I read. I didn't have to worry about taking her into a library. She never made a fuss.

By this time she was eight months old and she wasn't sitting up by herself. She wasn't even attempting to sit up. And her only attempt at crawling was to lie flat on her tummy and try to pull herself along with her arms. No matter how many times I put her up on her hands and knees and simulated the crawling motion with her, she didn't grasp the idea. She simply plopped down on her stomach.

So, again, I addressed this latest concern with Dr. Hampton. And, I reminded him that Stephanie was still sleeping too much. She was still too content to sit and do nothing.

"Hmm, you new mothers. Just because you have one very bright and active child, you think every other child has to be just as bright and just as active. Every child is different. You should be glad she sleeps instead of crying all of the time." He folded his arms across his chest and moved towards his desk, shaking his head.

"So, she's a little slow physically. She'll catch up, and then you'll wish that she was still lying around on the floor instead of getting into everything." In his usual gruff and demeaning manner, Dr. Hampton was dismissing my latest concern. He sat down at his desk.

"But, Dr. Hampton, when you add up the things that I've pointed out, don't you think I should be just *a little* concerned? Shouldn't you be concerned?" The exasperation and impatience showing plainly in my voice got his attention.

Raising his head from the folder in which he was recording the data from Stephanie's visit, he gently placed his pen on his desk. Peering through his thick, dark glasses, he nodded.

"I can understand why you have questions, but I honestly believe that Stephanie will catch up to her sister. Yes, she does seem a little behind on her gross motor skills, but I see hundreds of children who get a slow start in life and then roar past those who were in the 99th or 100th percentile in the beginning of their lives."

As I drove home, I reminded myself that I *must* stop overreacting to everything that Stephanie *wasn't* doing.

If only I could be as cavalier as Dr. Hampton. If only I *could truly* convince myself that we had nothing to worry about.

Now, as we sat in the hospital waiting room, after all those years, a disturbing uneasiness settled over me. Concern? More than concern.

The examination in the emergency room didn't take long. Stephanie, sitting on the long, narrow table covered with a sheet of white paper, squirmed and watched the doctor's every move, fearing that he would give her a shot. But, other than the bumps and bruises, obviously caused by the fall and the thrashing about, he could find nothing that indicated *why* she had had the seizures. She should undergo tests that would likely uncover the reason, he said. Again, we were reminded: *people don't have seizures for no reason.*

To love for the sake of being loved is human,
But to love for the sake of loving is angelic.

Alphonse Marie de Lamartine

"Well, there you . . . are. I was beginning . . . to wonder . . . what happened . . . to you. I didn't think . . . you wouldn't come, . . . but I didn't think . . . you'd be this . . . late either." Mom's words came out in punctuated gasps as we walked into her hospital room. She was holding her arm in the air, pointing to her wristwatch. "I've . . . been waiting . . . and watching." The oxygen machine thumped with each release of air.

Emphysema and its complications were devastating to watch.

For the past two years, Mom had lived in a nursing home where she could receive constant care and medication. It wasn't that none of us wanted to care for her in our homes; it was just that we were not equipped to handle the many needs that she had. She was no longer ambulatory, she was hooked up to an oxygen machine, and she had a long list of medications that had to be administered daily.

I leaned over the bed railing and kissed her sunken, pallid cheek. She smelled of Jergen's lotion and Ludens cough drops.

"I'm sorry we made you wait."

She was squinting, trying to shade her eyes from the glare of the sun that streaked through the open window blind and bounced off her glasses. I moved around the bed and pulled the cord to close the blind.

I smiled as I recalled the many times that Stephanie and I arrived at Mom's mobile home, ready to take her with us for the weekend. She would be sitting by the window, her clothes packed in brown paper shopping bags. My siblings and I jokingly called those bags Mom's luggage. It didn't matter that she had a suitcase in her closet. She preferred h*er luggage*. And always she told me how she had been waiting and watching for me.

My sister Lorraine, who lived next door to Mom, and I would exchange knowing glances. Though she was supposed to be expecting me around 4:30 in the afternoon, Mom would be ready by 8 o'clock in the morning, staring out the window, jingling her keys.

Now, Mom was clutching Stephanie close, asking her if she wanted a cough drop. Mom always had paper hankies in one hand and a box of cough drops in the other.

Stephanie always had a Dr Pepper with her.

"We had to stop by the ER. Stephanie fell off a chair, so we wanted to have her checked out." I continued my lie.

"Oh, no." Mom pulled Stephanie even closer, kissing her cheek and pulling her head down on her chest. She stroked her back.

Mom's rail-thin body barely made a swell under the sheet or a dent in the mattress. Her short gray hair was pushed up in a peak where her head met the pillow. Plastic tubing that penetrated up into her nostrils, ran across her cheeks, circled around her ears and hooked up to the oxygen machine that sat on the floor next to the bed. The tubing left a streak of pink depressions on the faded, careworn skin that covered her gaunt, drawn face.

"So, how are you feeling today?" I asked her. "You're looking good." Considering that this was just one of many rushed trips to the hospital because of her inability to breathe, she did look better than when she had arrived at the hospital four days ago.

"The doctor told me . . . that I can go . . . home soon, if my oxygen . . . level stays up." A faint smile played around her mouth.

I knew what she was thinking. The nursing home was not her home. Two years before, when she had to go into the home, we promised that we would try to get her out of there as soon as possible. At that point, I think we all knew that she would never return to her house, but I knew there would always be that glimmer of hope in her heart.

The next half-hour was spent watching Mom and Stephanie interacting. Their love for each other lit up the room. I often thought it wouldn't matter if *I* ever visited with my mother as long as I made sure Stephanie got there. In the two years that Mom was at the home, and in the hospital periodically, Steph and I had rarely missed a day of visiting. "Put your hand . . . on top . . . of my hand, and I'll put . . . my hand on top . . . of yours before . . . you can . . . pull your hand out. Ow! You made me . . . slap my own hand. You're just . . . too fast for me." Mom feigned injury while Stephanie laughed triumphantly.

They played silly games, sang silly songs, said silly rhymes, teased and taunted and just savored every minute together.

My heart warmed watching them. Stephanie, being as short as she was, stood at eye-level for Mom as she half-laid, half-sat in her hospital bed. Mischief and love made a pathway between their eyes.

But, I wondered, how much longer will they have to be best buddies? Mom's trips to the hospital were getting closer together and more ominous. Each time we spoke to her doctor he was less encouraging.

And now this added worry. What would Stephanie's MRI show? What if Stephanie wasn't going to be here for Mom to play with and love?

I had never thought about it that way before. Always I had worried that something would happen to Mom.

"Let Gramma . . . catch her . . . breath." She and Stephanie had just finished reciting "*Peter Piper . . . picked a peck . . . of pickled peppers,*" and deep wheezing sounds were coming from Mom's chest. Now her speech was even slower and more labored and her pale face took on a gray pallor.

I rang for the nurse. Mom needed more help than she was getting from the oxygen machine.

After the nurse gave her a shot and left with her tray of medications, I watched Mom. She closed her eyes and rested her head against the pillow, and I chattered on about the weather, the impending start of school, and a variety of mundane topics, while I watched her face and listened to her breathing. Gradually, her shallow breathing smoothed out and her face lost its gray pallor.

The sun had shifted, so I opened the blinds, letting the daylight brighten the room. "Mom, we need to leave now so you'll get some rest. We'll see you tomorrow." I adjusted her pillow, kissed her on the forehead, and rested my hand inside hers.

She raised her frail, thin arm and squeezed my hand against her face. "Well, I thank you . . . for coming because . . . I know how busy . . . you are." Tears welled in her eyes and her lips quivered.

I ducked my head and hugged her. I didn't want her to see the tears that were threatening to spill down my face. "Mom, I've told you so many times. You don't have to thank me for visiting you. I want to visit you." I struggled to control my quavering voice as I kept my face hidden in the crook of her neck.

It had never hit me as hard as it did that day. Yes, I would miss my Mom terribly, and yes, I loved her dearly, but how would Stephanie react to losing her? She would never understand death.

How would Mom react to losing Stephanie? Stephanie was Mom's lifeline to the past. She could play the same games, sing the same songs, and say the same rhymes that she had done with all of us when we were kids. Stephanie warmed Mom's heart in a way that none of us could as adults.

How would I react to losing either one of them? I couldn't bear the thought.

Why was I even thinking such things? Stephanie had a seizure. Nothing more. Mom always bounced back from her hospital stays.

As Ronnie drove home, an uncomfortable silence settled over us. I supposed we were both worrying about Mom and Stephanie. I glanced over my shoulder into the back seat where Stephanie was holding George and chiding him for not going to sleep.

Curious George was as human to Stephanie as any child was to its mother. George had a bassinet, a stroller, and more outfits than any one of us owned. His clothes took up more drawer space in Stephanie's room than hers did. She dressed him, undressed him, fed him, changed his diaper, rocked him, loved him, scolded him, and tended to his every imagined need. The only advantage that I could see that she had over any mother with a real child was that if she didn't feel like taking care of him, she would just announce that George wasn't feeling well, so he would be spending the day in bed.

"Steph, honey, how is George doing? Has he been sick lately?" I figured there must be something wrong with him, since she hadn't taken him into the hospital to visit with Gramma.

"Nah, he's fine. I'm just gettin' tired of carryin' him around. He's gonna' hafta learn to walk. I guess I'll start teachin' him tomorrow." She snuggled him in her arms and began rocking back and forth.

I hoped that her efforts to get George to walk were easier than what we had experienced just to *get to* the walking phase of Stephanie's life.

Eventually Stephanie did learn to sit up by herself, but it was a long, hard struggle for her. Every day, several times a day, I sat her in front of the sofa, surrounded by pillows, front, back and sides, stacked as high as her shoulders. My theory was that, if I could get her to sit up long enough, her muscles would strengthen and she would develop a sense of balance.

At first, she would lose her balance and wobble from side to side, causing the pillows to push far enough away to allow her to topple over. I would sit her up straight, over and over again, restack the pillows and start the process once more. Eventually, when I thought she had enough control to stay upright for a length of time, I would remove the top row of pillows, making her work harder to sit up without support. Over a period of several weeks, she could sit up with just one row of pillows, and finally she could sit without any support. Her triumphant smile, sparkling eyes, and clapping hands told me she was very proud of herself.

She never did master the conventional crawl, but she did manage to get where she wanted to go by pulling herself along with her arms. I reminded myself that I wasn't going to get upset about what Stephanie didn't do, but instead, I was going to appreciate everything that she did do.

On her first birthday, we invited family and friends to celebrate with us. While Stephanie didn't seem to know why we were all gathered together, she was fascinated by the brightly-colored packages that were piled next to her on the floor in the middle of the family room. She slapped her hands on the top of the pile and babbled happily. Her young cousins encouraged her to pull the bows from the packages and tear the paper from the boxes that hid her gifts. She was enjoying all of the attention, but she made no attempt to open the packages by herself. Robyn was happy to help her.

"Is Stephanie pulling herself up to the furniture and trying to walk yet?" My brother-in-law, Dominic, followed me into the kitchen when I went to get the cake.

An innocent enough question, but it renewed the nagging thoughts and fears that hung in the edges of my mind. Really I didn't expect her to be walking yet, and I had to admit that I would be surprised if she tried to pull herself up because she wasn't even crawling. But, I reasoned, I did know of some children who never crawled; they just went directly into walking. And, Robyn didn't walk until she was fifteen months old. Then, again, Robyn didn't exhibit any of the many other difficulties that Stephanie had been displaying since birth.

Despite all of Dr. Hampton's reassurances, I did worry that Stephanie was too content to sit for long periods of time just watching me as I made beds, sorted laundry, prepared meals, or any number of other chores I might be doing. I would carry her to where I was working, sit her where she could see me as I moved from one part of the room to another, and she followed me with her eyes, smiling when I looked at her. She didn't fuss, she didn't attempt to crawl; she didn't pay much attention to the toys that I carried from room to room and placed on her lap. She just *watched* me.

"No, she hasn't tried that yet," I told my brother-in-law. "But Dr. Hampton doesn't seem to be concerned. And I have to keep remembering that Robyn was a late walker." I smiled and walked back into the family room, carrying the cake with one burning candle, gratefully losing myself in the commotion of adult chatter and kids playing.

While Stephanie's motor skills were obviously delayed, she began communicating to us and with us at a reasonable pace. She said the usual Da Da and Ma Ma, and a few other words that I repeated over and over as she sat on my lap and I read to her. "Say book, say dog, say cat, say boy, say girl," I prompted.

True, she didn't form complete sentences, but she reacted to our requests and obeyed commands when we spoke to her. She pointed to objects and people that we asked her to identify, she recognized and identified colors, and she responded appropriately when we asked her a yes or no question. But her unusual contentment that bordered on indifference was a constant source of stress.

Busy. Busy. Don't think. Don't think.

By January, when Stephanie was eighteen months old, she still was not walking, but she had begun to try to pull up to the furniture. She would get as far as her knees, so Ronnie and I would stand her up on her feet and try to get her to hold on and walk around the coffee table. She would lift her tiny foot, try to move it forward, and then collapse onto the floor. It was apparent that she understood what she was supposed to do, but it just wasn't working. We would pick her up, place her tiny hands on the edge of the table, and she would try again. Again she would fall. We repeated the process over and over.

By the middle of February, it was obvious to both of us that Stephanie was not going to be able to walk on her own, and we couldn't figure out why, since she clearly understood the procedure.

I couldn't sleep. My mind was full of questions and concerns but no answers. I huddled under the covers in a fetal position, staring at the wall, wishing that Stephanie had been able to do the conventional crawl, wishing that she'd wake up tomorrow and fuss and cry when I sat her on the floor in the middle of a room, wishing she would play with the toys that I placed on her lap, wishing that she would be able to walk, wishing that her indifference would change into interest and curiosity, wishing it would all go away.

When I woke up the next morning, I knew what I had to do.

"Stephanie's due for a booster shot this month, so I'm going to tell Dr. Hampton that we want to see a specialist about her not being able to walk. I'm tired of him putting me off every time I have a concern." I sat on the edge of the bed, holding Stephanie, while Ronnie dressed for school. "I think it has gone way beyond just being a late developer. If he can't, or won't, do anything for Stephanie, then he needs to send us to someone who can and will." I could feel the anger, mixed with fear, swelling inside me. As much as I wanted to go on believing that there wasn't anything wrong, I couldn't deny it any longer. I had hid behind Dr. Hampton's ineffectual explanations long enough.

"Do you want me to go with you?" I could hear the uneasiness in Ronnie's voice. "I don't mind." He knotted his tie in front of the dresser mirror.

"I know, but you'd better save your days in case we need them later."

Already I sensed the troubles that we might be facing.

That afternoon, the waiting room was full of people. Panic set in. If I had to wait a long time to see Dr. Hampton, would I lose my nerve? I concentrated on the small window next to the receptionist's desk. The wind was blowing a bare tree branch against the glass making a scratching noise. I would count the number of scratches on the window pane while I waited. I wouldn't think about what I wanted to say. What I *had* to say.

The pain from the shot was momentary, and Stephanie's tears were subsiding. I couldn't put it off any longer.

I took a deep, ragged breath and began. "Dr. Hampton, I know that we've talked about this before, but Stephanie still isn't walking. Now, I know that you reminded me that she could catch up to all of those other children in the 99th and 100th percentile, and I know that Robyn was a late walker, and I know that you think I'm overly concerned about Stephanie's development, but I think we need to do something for her. Now." There.

I'd said it. I wasn't sure if he understood everything I said, because the words had gushed out of my mouth, but I knew if I didn't say it fast, I'd never get it done.

I took a deep breath and walked over to his desk with Stephanie straddling my hip.

"She does pull herself up to the coffee table, and she does try to take steps, but she keeps falling down. No matter how many times she does it, she keeps falling down. I know she understands what she's supposed to do, but she can't." By now my voice was shaking and tears were welling in my eyes. I took another deep breath and stared into his thick, dark glasses. My heart was pounding, and my hands were sweating.

I couldn't tell if it was irritation or amazement that covered his face. I'd never said that much to him in all the years that we had been his patients. At least not all at one time. Slowly, he pulled himself from his chair. "Well, if you feel that strongly about it, maybe we should do something to ease your mind."

Darn him. Why did he always make me feel like my concerns were unwarranted? Why was he always condescending in his responses to me? Why was I never right and he was never wrong?

"Well, yes, I do think we should do something." I wasn't going to give any ground.

"Okay, let me set up an appointment with Dr. James. He's an orthopedist. Maybe he'll have the answers you're looking for. I'll have his office contact you." He sat back down at his desk, lowered his head and began writing in his file. He was miffed. How dare I question his judgment?

My hands were shaking as I gripped the steering wheel and turned left out of the parking lot. Thoughts were spinning around in my head like the small flakes of snow that were swirling in the wind but not sticking to the windshield or the road.

Every area of trouble gives out a ray of hope, and the one unchangeable certainty is that nothing is certain or unchangeable.

I read the small plaque that hung on the wall opposite my chair.

It was a quote from John F. Kennedy; a quote I clung to as I sat in the small examination room with Stephanie waiting for Dr. James. Yes, we were entering into an *area of trouble*, but I would cling to the *ray of hope* that whatever we faced would be *changeable*.

There was a light tap on the door, and Dr. James came into the examination room.

"Well, Stephanie, don't you have beautiful blue eyes. They match your dress. Or does your dress match your eyes?" He patted Stephanie on the head and carried her towards a small wooden desk sitting in the corner of the room. He motioned for me to sit in the chair facing him.

The soft music playing in the background was soothing and tranquil. I felt comfortable and safe in my new medical world.

"Tell me about Stephanie and the problems that she has when she tries to walk." He sat in his swivel chair with Stephanie on his lap. She'd found a container of pens and pencils on the desk and was busily scribbling on a yellow legal pad.

I folded Stephanie's coat and placed it on a chair next to me. "Well, this is just the latest in a long list of things that we've been concerned about since Steph was born. It seems to us that she knows how to walk, how to move her legs and feet, but every time she steps forward, she falls down."

"You say you have a list of things that concern you?" Dr. James crossed his long legs and bounced Stephanie up and down to her delight.

Wow, I thought. He's actually interested in what I have to say. I cleared my throat, leaned forward in my chair and started recounting every visit and every conversation that I'd had with Dr. Hampton from Stephanie's birth up to the present.

Dr. James, listening intently, nodded occasionally, frowned occasionally, and raised his eyebrows occasionally. His wire-rimmed glasses were perched on the end of his nose. He ran his fingers through his thinning hair.

For the first time, I felt that I was being taken seriously, and what I had to say was important. I didn't feel rushed. I didn't feel ignored. I didn't feel dismissed.

When I finished, he carried Stephanie to the examination table and began prodding and probing around her hips, rolling her from side to side. She reached out for me, but she didn't cry.

Isn't he going to say something, I wondered? Is he going to give me the run around too? Was I fooled by his kind and fatherly nature? *Am* I just an over-anxious mother?

He finished his examination, returned to his desk and wrote on a small pad. "We'll get some pictures of Stephanie's hips, and we should have the answers we need before you leave today." He patted Stephanie on the head, walked to the door, and signaled for his nurse.

An answer.

Yes. Yes. Yes. It wasn't that I wanted there to be something wrong with Steph; I just wanted some answers. I wanted someone to see what Ronnie and I saw everyday. I wanted someone to help us.

A half—hour later, Dr. James walked into the room, dropped his folder of x ray pictures on top of a file cabinet and perched himself on the edge of his desk. "Before I give you all of the medical jargon that goes with my diagnosis, just let me say, in layman's terms, that Stephanie has a malformation of the hip bones, which causes them to fall out of place every time that she stands up." He made a gesture with his index fingers demonstrating how the bones failed to lock into her hips. "Hence, the falling down and not being able to stand alone and walk."

"She'll never be able to walk?" The words sprang from my mouth. I clutched Stephanie against my chest and cradled her head against my neck.

This wasn't what I had expected. My heart pounded and the blood drained from my face. This wasn't what I had hoped for. My arms began to shake and I pressed Stephanie's head tighter against my neck.

"Oh yes, she'll walk. It'll just take some time and some help from braces." He slid off the edge of his desk, smiled and touched my arm, recognizing that I had misunderstood.

"We'll get everything scheduled for the fitting of the brace, and before you know it, she'll be scooting around the house getting into everything."

I exhaled in relief and collapsed into a chair. "Oh thank you so much. I knew there was a reason why she didn't walk. I knew I was right. I mean, I knew it wasn't that she didn't know how or just didn't want to walk. I mean, I knew it wasn't just that . . ." I stopped in mid-sentence. I was rambling on. I was so comforted by his encouraging words. I wasn't just an over-anxious mother. There really was something wrong with Steph.

And then reality coursed through my body like a wave washing ashore. It meant there *was* something wrong with Steph. Oh no, I cried inwardly, I don't want to be right if Steph has to have something wrong with her.

And then another thought equally devastating. Since I was right about her inability to walk . . . then . . . was I right about all of her problems? Did they all point towards, and even worse, beyond developmental delays? What was the saying that I had heard once? *Be careful what you wish for, you just might get it*. I had wished for answers, but not the answers I received.

"Rest assured that we will do everything we can to make Stephanie walk as soon as it's physically and medically possible. I know that you're nervous and anxious, but I don't want you and your husband to worry unnecessarily. We will have her walking." He turned to his desk, sat down, and picked up an envelope.

I smiled weakly and nodded.

"However, there is one more thing that concerns me. I have debated with myself about whether to tell you or not. But, after having listened to what you have experienced with Dr. Hampton, and having visually and physically examined Stephanie, I have decided that I *must* show you this letter." He pulled a paper from the envelope.

In one quick motion, he thrust the letter into my hand and lifted Stephanie from my arms and onto his lap.

Bewildered, I focused on the heading of the letter. It was from Dr. Hampton.

I began reading. Dazed, I allowed the words to sink in. . . . *insists on seeing a specialist . . . young and over-anxious mother . . . has one quick, bright, child . . . a worrier . . . told her that late developers can catch up . . . do what you can to placate her . . .*

In stunned disbelief, clutching the letter in my shaking hand, I lowered it into my lap. Tears streaked down my face. I felt betrayed. I felt belittled. I felt degraded. I felt . . . "I can't believe that he would . . ." My heart was thundering in my ears. I stood up and leaned on the examination table.

"I find that listening to mothers often makes my job easier. Mothers have an innate sense when it comes to raising their children. There's a bond, or a connection, if you will, that helps mothers know when all is not well." He shifted Stephanie to his other knee.

"Not only is Dr. Hampton demonstrating gross insensitivity, his letter is highly unethical and unprofessional. I *will* report this to the medical board of ethics. And from my perspective, Dr. Hampton's inaction is inexcusable." His voice took on an air of indignant consternation.

"I empathize with you and your husband for all that you've been through. From what you've told me and from what little I have observed today, I *do believe* that your concerns are justified. I *do believe* that Stephanie has some developmental issues."

'Your concerns are justified. Your concerns are justified.' Those words played over and over in my mind on the drive home.

'Stephanie has some developmental issues.' I had wanted someone to recognize what I'd been pointing out all along, and now that Dr. James verified my fears, I was almost angry with him. I'd never felt such ambivalence as I was experiencing right then.

I didn't want something to be wrong with Stephanie. I had just wanted someone to listen to me. I had just wanted someone to believe me. I had just wanted it all to go away.

Later, as I sat on the edge of the bed holding Stephanie, and related the contents of the letter to Ronnie, the look on his face told me that he was as angry and frustrated as I was. "Did he think that Dr. James would just accept what he said and not react professionally?" I could see the veins in his neck pulsing, a familiar indication that his anger was building. "You'll *never* set foot in his office again."

He paced back and forth, from the bed to the dresser, spewing his words in his deep baritone voice. "He's nothing but a quack. Even if you don't think your patients are right, you don't belittle them by writing a derogatory letter to another doctor." He ripped the knot out of his tie, yanked it from around his neck, and threw it on the pale blue, wing—back chair next to the window.

"And the worst part of it is, he's wrong." He crumpled his shirt into a ball and threw it on the chair with his tie, angry darts flashing from his eyes. "No, the worst part is that he wasted so much time that we could've been doing something about Steph's problems." His features softened and his eyes lost their anger as he reached down and took Stephanie into his arms.

I stood and walked to the window, staring at the aging gray barn that divided the yard and the circle driveway from the open fields that soon would be covered with corn and wheat.

"We should sue him," I said. "If we took him to court, we'd probably win."

But, as I ranted on about what we should do, I knew in my heart that we'd do nothing. My timid, insecure, unworldly self wouldn't have the courage to engage in a confrontation with a doctor. And Ronnie, in deference to me, wouldn't cause a fuss either.

Two weeks later, sitting in the waiting room at the children's orthopedic hospital, I had a feeling of well-being. We had support. We were not out there floundering around by ourselves.

Except for the chairs that the adults sat in, the room was filled with miniature furniture to accommodate the children. Multi—colored plastic chairs surrounded a matching-colored plastic table; miniature cabinets, stoves and sinks lined one wall.

A small boy crawled around on the floor playing with miniature cars, dragging his braced leg behind him, while a girl, older and bigger than Stephanie, sat at a table feeding a doll baby plastic food from plastic dishes and spoons, her one arm braced from the elbow to the wrist.

Stephanie chattered and pointed at the brightly colored walls that were painted with pictures of animals. "Doggie. Kitty-cat. Bunny. Horsy." Her voice raised in excitement as she recognized the animals that she saw in her books.

When she tired of identifying animals, she spotted a box of toys sitting in the corner of the room and strained and squirmed to get off my lap. I carried her across the room and sat her on the play mat, surrounding her with Teddy bears, baby dolls, and books. She clapped her hands, her blue eyes flashing in anticipation.

Later, as we sat in the examination room, a balding, pot-bellied doctor burst through the door, exuding confidence, smiled at Stephanie, placed a folder on a metal desk, and said, "Let's get started." His voice was assertive and energetic.

I liked his no—nonsense attitude. After the formal exchange of names, he offered us seats, talked to us as though he believed that what we said had some validity, and listened to us like he cared about what we had to say. Okay, I thought, we're headed in the right direction.

"Hi, Stephanie. I'm going to help you take off your clothes and let you wear a special gown. What do you think of that?" The nurse started unbuttoning Stephanie's blouse.

Stephanie's lower lip quivered as she reached for me. "It's okay," I assured her, "Mommy and Daddy will be right here with you."

Yes, I thought, let's get started.

I thought of this now, all these years later as Ronnie pulled the car into the garage. Stephanie had fallen asleep clutching George to her chest. It had been a long and frightening day. The seizures had tired her out. And besides, she had to save her energy; she was going to teach George to walk tomorrow. Ronnie scooped her up in his arms and carried her into the house.

With the initial shock of Stephanie's seizures wearing off, I began to recall the days and weeks leading up to that frightening moment. At the time I didn't think much about it, but Stephanie had been complaining of headaches throughout the spring and summer. I attributed the headaches to her allergy to pollen, which caused her nose to run and her eyes to turn red and weep, and I gave her the medicines that Dr. Thompson, our family doctor, had prescribed. But, now, I thought, perhaps something more serious was going on inside of her head. Perhaps her susceptibility to allergies had led us in the wrong direction.

"I can't add much more to what the doctors at the hospital have told you, but I will prescribe a common anti-seizure medication until we can get an MRI." Dr. Thompson had finished his examination and was moving around his small office looking for his prescription pad.

"And we need to weigh her and make sure I give her the right dosage. It looks like she's lost some weight."

As Stephanie stood on the scale, an unexpected eerie, uneasy sense of foreboding crept through my body. I had noticed the weight loss, but her energy level seemed to be fine. And she had never been a big eater. And it had been a very hot summer. Who feels like eating when it's hot? I had reasoned it all away.

But now, I realized, her headaches that didn't seem to be helped with her allergy medicine, her weight loss, and her seizures surely were indicators that there was something going on inside of Stephanie. Why didn't I recognize it before now? Why did it take three different incidents bunched together to awaken me to the possibility that there was something wrong? I could feel my face flushing and my body felt clammy and hot at the same time. Why had I overlooked the warning signals? What had happened to this innate sense, this bond, this connection that mothers have when it comes to their children? Where did I put it? When did I lose it?

If you weren't a patient in the hospital, and you weren't being brought into the hospital as an emergency case, it was difficult to get an appointment for an MRI. We were told that it would be over a month before they could schedule Stephanie. That wasn't good news, but it wasn't that bad either. Stephanie appeared to be fine. She hadn't had a seizure since she'd started the medication.

By now, it was nearing the time for all of us to get back into our school-year routine. Ronnie would be starting his twenty-third year at the local community college, and I would be going back into the classroom to teach English to high school students.

Stephanie, as part of a school program, had, for years, been working at a nearby veterans' hospital, cleaning rooms and hallways, with the help and guidance of her friend, Mary Lee. But since she had turned twenty-one, four years ago, and graduated with a certificate of attendance and had to leave the school program, she was now going to the college with Ronnie each day.

Having to leave the veteran's hospital and Mary Lee was made easier by Professor Carroll Mitchell. When Stephanie wasn't sitting in on Ronnie's classes, she was helping Carroll grade papers.

Carroll, a psychology professor, arranged her office so that Stephanie would have room for her desk and chair. Stephanie accumulated stacks of papers, colored pencils, scissors, paper clips, rubber bands, and personal objects that clearly identified the space as hers. George sat on her desk, along side her Mickey Mouse cup, her wallet full of food coupons clipped from the inserts in the *Baltimore Sun*, and her favorite Smurf. And, of course, there was always a note she had written to give to

Carroll. Her notes usually told Carroll that she loved and missed her and often talked about her plans to write a play about Mickey Mouse.

At first, Stephanie missed her days of working at the veterans' hospital. She especially missed the time that she could spend with Mary Lee, a kind, nurturing middle—aged woman who mopped, dusted, scrubbed and straightened up the many rooms and hallways in the hospital. Stephanie tagged along and helped. Mary's patience with, and love for, Stephanie, radiated from her warm brown eyes the first time that we met. She included Stephanie in everything she did at work. She helped her navigate the steps, she showered her with small gifts, mostly pins, necklaces, and rings from her own personal belongings. It thrilled Stephanie to have something that Mary Lee had worn.

Mary's most distinguishing trait was the vivid colored flowers that she wore in her long, dark hair every day. And those flowers depicted her personality; bright and cheerful. But more significant to Stephanie was Mary's child-like enthusiastic approach to life. Working with Mary was not work. Working with Mary was laughter, excitement, anticipation, and a lunch-hour scheduled around their favorite soap opera.

Stephanie had started working in the program at the veteran's hospital as a volunteer, but eventually they began to pay her. She was elated. It meant more money to spend on George. Every Friday night began with pizza at Pappy's restaurant and ended at the toy store in the mall. Never would she have spent the amount of time shopping for her own clothes that she spent shopping for George's clothes and toys.

She also spent equal amounts of time hunting for a puzzle that she didn't already own. Her expertise with puzzles allowed her to finish putting together the one she would buy that very evening. The puzzles she selected always had more than one hundred pieces, but not more than two hundred and fifty, and most always they were pictures of animals, especially cats. After putting the puzzle together in the routine method of working from the outside edges to the middle, she would get bored and work from the opposite direction. The puzzles were no longer a challenge after a day or two.

Clearly, it would do her good to get back to the college campus and busy herself with Professor Mitchell and the rest of her friends.

Jennifer, our youngest daughter would also be going back to the local community college to complete her second year. She would continue to live at home, much to her chagrin. It just wasn't cool to live at home when you were in college. And it certainly wasn't cool to go to the college where your father was a professor, and it was far too easy for him to keep tabs on her grades and her behavior.

When I learned that I was pregnant with Jennifer, I waffled between times of happiness and anxiety. I continually asked myself *what if* . . . What if this precious baby was physically and mentally handicapped? What if Stephanie's mental and physical defects were genetic? The question that kept haunting me was: Could we care for two physically and mentally handicapped children? The *what ifs* surrounded and smothered me.

I prayed. I worried. I fretted. I prayed.

Finally, I decided that I would not give in to the apprehension that was attempting to swallow me. I would look forward to this baby just as I had the first two. Maybe this baby would be the boy that I had been sure I was going to have with the previous pregnancies. Maybe this baby would be the football quarterback that I wanted.

Or, maybe this baby would be physically and mentally handicapped, and I would love and cherish it like I did Robyn and Stephanie.

For the remaining seven months of my pregnancy my emotions fluctuated like the weather, but I kept my worries and concerns to myself. To the outside world, I was just another expectant mother. Inside I was a churning, whirling, smoldering bundle of emotions, happy and expectant one moment and worried and fearful the next.

Time went by too fast. Time went by too slow.

The nurse placed the pink bundle into my arms, and I couldn't believe what I was seeing. I had a thumb sucker. I always thought it was so cute when babies sucked their thumbs, so I had tried unsuccessfully to get both Robyn and Stephanie to suck their thumbs. And here, without any prompting, was our thumb sucker.

And then my fears snuffed out any pleasure: Was she going to be normal? Would she have any obvious defects?

Hesitantly, I pulled the pink blanket away from her tiny body. Would I find something even more obvious than an indentation? I inspected her from head to toe. Everything seemed to be perfectly developed and perfectly placed. My heart swelled with love for our Jennifer Elizabeth. I snuggled and cuddled her, and kissed her soft, warm neck. She would be okay. I just knew it. She would *not* be physically and mentally handicapped.

When they took her back to the nursery, an uneasy uncertainty crept through my mind. I hadn't entirely convinced myself that she would be okay, so I hurried to the nursery and watched her through the glass partition. I had to know. Was she moving her arms and legs? Was she looking around? Was she crying? Was she doing all of the things that Stephanie hadn't done?

Yes.

I waited anxiously for the nurse to return her to me.

Again, I examined her tiny, sweet-smelling body. I ran my hand over the base of her skull. No indentation. I scrutinized her eyes. No visible unevenness. She's going to be okay, I assured myself. Already her bright gray-green eyes were alertly staring at the overhead lights, and her pudgy, active fingers clamored to grab my cheeks. I said a silent prayer of thanks.

Throughout the next seven months, I found myself watching for signs that might show that Jennifer would be handicapped in some way, but there were no indications. She was sitting up without support, she was doing the conventional crawl, and she was alert and aware of everything that was going on. She *would* be okay.

And now she was a sophomore in college.

A week had gone by, and Stephanie hadn't had another seizure. The medicine was working. Now I could concentrate on getting our schedules organized for the start of the school—year.

Stephanie was far more excited about the new school year than any of us. She liked and trusted everyone and assumed that everyone liked her and that she could trust everyone. All through the years, that was one concern that we dealt with no matter where Stephanie went. She was innocent and child-like in her relationships. It never occurred to her that anyone would, or could, be mean or a threat to her. Her world was far different from the one we lived in.

We didn't want her to think that we were hovering over her, but we kept a very close eye on her. If Ronnie, Robyn, Jennifer, or I wasn't with her, we made sure that she was being monitored by someone we trusted.

Every professor, custodian, secretary, most of the students, and even the deans and president of the college knew her. She spoke to everyone.

There were times when she was a bit outspoken. Once, when we had had a snow storm, and the college parking lot was still slushy and slick, she and Ronnie met up with the president of the college as they were walking into the building. "Dr. Grant, you'd better get some of your men out here to scrape this mess off of this parking lot. Someone's gonna fall and get hurt." Stephanie shook her skinny, slightly crooked, index finger in a firm reprimand.

Dr. Grant smiled, and said, "Okay, Stephanie, I'll see to it right now."

Another time, shortly before Christmas, when Stephanie was in the Student Center, a very tall young man went over to the Christmas tree, took an ornament, hooked it over his ear, and proudly displayed it to his fellow basketball players.

Stephanie, all four feet of her, hurried over and stood in front of this giant-of-a-young man. With her hands on her hips, she demanded, "You put that right back on the tree. It doesn't belong to you."

Without hesitation, or comment, he hastily made his way back to the tree and replaced the ornament. She would be fine at the college with Ronnie.

But this was the first day that I'd been away from Stephanie since her seizures began, and I couldn't get her out of my mind. I sat in the library with the rest of the faculty trying to focus on what our principal was saying. I stared at the rows of books on the shelves, fidgeted in my chair, flipped through the school discipline manual, scribbled on the edges of the agenda sheet, and scanned the room, searching for the new teachers' faces, but nothing I did would free my mind from worrying about Stephanie.

Was the seizure medication still working? If she should have a seizure at the college, would she be frightened? Would she cry for me? And, by stopping the seizures, what was the medicine covering up?

I forced myself to listen, but I couldn't wait for the beginning-of-school faculty meetings to be over so that I could go home and see for myself that Stephanie was okay.

Once home, I hurried into the living room. As usual Ronnie was reading the newspaper and Stephanie was hiding. "Where's Stephanie?" I pretended that I didn't see her huddled in the corner of the sofa with her face buried in a pillow.

"I don't know." Ronnie joined in with the pretense.

"Did you go to the college and leave her there?" I made my voice rise in mock terror.

"I don't think I left her there. I thought she was in the car with me."

"Oh boy, I guess we'll have to get back to the college and hunt for her. Come on, get your keys." I turned, pretending to hurry towards the door.

"I'm here! I'm here! I came home!" Stephanie clamored off the sofa and rushed to my side, throwing her arms around me.

I hugged her close. "Oh, I'm so glad you're here. You really scared me. What would I ever do without you?"

A brief, unsettling, twinge of fear coursed through my body. *What would I ever do without her?*

Stephanie pranced in delight over her perceived deception. We'd been playing this game since she was old enough to grasp the concept of hiding. However, she never quite understood that just because she covered her face and couldn't see me, I could still see her.

I breathed a sigh of relief. She had gone to the college with Ronnie, her medicine obviously worked, and I had made it through a day without her.

"Did you teach George to walk today," I asked? George was nowhere in sight.

"Nah. He kept fallin' down every time I let go of his hands, so I jus' quit. Then Dad 'n' I had to go to the college, so I put him to bed. How did you teach me to walk, Mommy?"

"No, no, no!" Stephanie screamed and cried while the therapists fitted the brace between her upper thighs and the doctor attempted to explain the process over the noise. Stephanie's tears, mixed with the mucus from her nose, were being spread all over her face as she balled her hands into tiny fists and rubbed them over her cheeks.

I was trying to listen to the doctor's explanation, but my mind and attention was focused on Stephanie. "Don't cry sweetheart. No one's going to hurt you. Mommy and Daddy are both here." I tried to stay far enough away not to interfere with the process, but I wanted to stroke her and make her feel safe.

"So, that's how the brace fits." He gave a tug on the metal bar, demonstrating that it wouldn't budge if it was fastened properly. "And remember that it has to stay on twenty-four hours a day. You only remove it to give Stephanie her bath. She must sleep in it." I could feel my face contorting into a look of surprise and pain.

Responding to my facial expression, he said, "If she *doesn't* sleep in it, what the brace manages to correct during the day will all be lost at night." Again, I could feel my face reacting to the thought of Stephanie having to wear this bulky, cumbersome brace day and night.

"I know it seems cruel, but she *will* get used to it. It'll bother you two far more than it will bother her." He tilted his head and raised his eyebrows in a sympathetic gesture.

Then smiling, as though he could read my mind, he said, "And believe it or not, as cumbersome as it seems, she will be able to move around in it. She'll look like a crab scooting around the floor, but she *will* get where she wants to go."

"Will she be in pain?" I stroked her hair while she continued to cry.

"Some, at first, but nothing that you can't control with baby aspirin." He watched Stephanie as she continued to struggle and fight the brace.

"Most of her tears will come from fear of what she doesn't understand. She'll adjust quickly." He shook our hands and reminded us that we could call him any time that we had questions or concerns. He would be responsible for Stephanie's care.

We wouldn't see Dr. James anymore. Would we ever find out if he sent Dr. Hampton's letter to the ethics board?

We set the time for our next appointment and readied to go home. Steph's legs were thrust away from her body so that her knees stuck out on either side of her. The metal brace, fastened to Stephanie's inner thighs, ran horizontally in the front of her. It not only looked awkward, but I was certain that it was painful, for she hadn't stopped crying since they had started putting it in place.

Stephanie cried the whole way home and continued crying throughout the night. We had started giving her baby aspirin as soon as we arrived home, but it didn't stop the tears. I guessed the doctor was right. She was crying more from fear than she was from pain.

With the brace thrust between her legs and jutting out in front of her, I couldn't hold her so that she was facing me, and I couldn't carry her around to soothe and comfort her, so I sat on the sofa with her sitting on my lap, facing away from me. I did the best I could to calm and console her, but she fought to turn around. She wanted to snuggle with me, but that was impossible while we were sitting up.

Well into the night I decided that she wasn't going to settle down, so I lay on my back on the floor, her legs spread on either side of me with the brace pushing into my stomach, her face nestled in my neck, her body resting securely where she wanted to be. She fell into a fitful sleep.

After a week of sleeping like this, I determined that this wasn't a good idea. Stephanie was going to want to spend all of her nights lying on top of me, and that could mean a year to eighteen months of lying on my back on the floor. So, as painful as it was, I put her into her crib, walked out and sat on the floor, in the hallway, next to her bedroom door, waiting for the tears to flow.

She wailed, she rolled back and forth, she banged her brace against the rails of the crib, she sobbed, she tossed from side to side, she sobbed, she banged her head against the headboard. She pleaded, "Mommy. Mommy."

I cried with her. I wanted to give in, rush through the door, pick her up, tell her how sorry I was, and beg her to forgive me for the pain that she was going through.

Finally, the wailing stopped, the sobs relented, the banging subsided, and her soft imploring voice silenced.

The next night, knowing what was going to happen when I carried her into her bedroom, she clung to my neck and begged, "No, Mommy, no."

Again, I sat outside her bedroom door, encased in guilt and pain, listening to the banging, tossing, rolling and pleading.

Abruptly and unexpectedly, there was silence. I could hear her soft, even breathing. She was asleep.

For several nights we followed the same pattern, and then one night she didn't cling to me, didn't wail, didn't bang, didn't roll, didn't plead, just said "Night, night," and went to sleep.

The days had been easier from the beginning. She busied herself with her coloring books, baby dolls, and spending time with me, reading her favorite stories. And she took naps lying beside me on our bed. Having Mommy right next to her was like healing medicine.

With Robyn getting down on the floor demonstrating how it should be done, it wasn't long before Stephanie, with her legs spread out on either side of her, her tiny feet barely touching the floor, her stomach thrust towards the ceiling, and her hands placed on the floor behind her shoulders for support, did everything but climb the stairs. She and Robyn had *crab* races, tearing through the living room into the dining room, circling the table and returning to the living room.

We had banged up dining room chair legs and scratched floors, but no one cared. Stephanie was on the move.

❧❦

Regret for the things we did can be tempered by time,
It is regret for the things we did not do that is inconsolable

Sidney J. Harris

❧❦

Back in school, I struggled to focus on my students, finding myself repeatedly thinking about Stephanie and how she was doing. Every time someone called my classroom on the intercom, I was sure it was about Stephanie. Nervously, I awaited a phone call from home or the college. I began to question why I was in school. Why wasn't I home with Stephanie?

But, then I would remind myself that so far all that had happened was a few seizures on a Sunday morning. Scary? Yes. But everything was under control now.

Then, just as quickly as I convinced myself that I was worrying needlessly, my thoughts would catapult me back into a state of nervous tension. I could ask myself over and over why I was so worried over a couple of seizures, but in my heart I knew why. Stephanie's past history did not bode well for these seizures to be inconsequential incidents.

Mom had returned to the nursing home and was doing *okay*. I say *okay* because she wasn't eating like she should to maintain her strength. "Mom," I would say each evening when we visited, "you have to eat if you want to get better." But we both knew this was a foolish statement. Mom would never get better. There were so many things I wanted to say to her and so many things I wanted to discuss, but I knew that putting my thoughts into words, made them more real, made them gain validity, and I didn't want this. I didn't want to face the obvious, the inevitable.

At one point, several weeks before Mom's last hospital stay, we began talking about sacred music. Mom always loved music. As kids, we grew up listening to polkas, to which Mom would dance and whoop it up, big band sounds, Southern gospel, church hymns, and any other music that Mom happened to find on our small radio with its scratchy reception. And, if she recognized the song, she would either sing along or whistle the tune. She was an accomplished whistler.

"We sang some beautiful songs in church this morning," I said.

"I love, *I Come to the Garden Alone*," she said softly. "When I die, I want people to sing that at my funeral." Her eyes began to water.

"Oh, Mom," I replied softly, blinking to keep the tears from streaming down my face. "You don't have to think about those things now." I reached for her thin, vein-ridden hand, absorbing the warmth.

"If not now, when?" Tears escaped down her pale, sunken cheeks.

I couldn't blink fast enough. Tears trickled down my cheeks, landing on top of our clenched hands. Now, I thought. Talk to her now about the many things that have been going on in your head. *Do it now.*

Stealthily, with my free hand, I reached for a tissue. "Okay, if you want that song, I'll make sure we sing it." Swiftly, I turned from the bedside and wiped my face. In a strained, but cheerful, voice, I continued, "So, is there any other song that you like?"

"I want, *How Great Thou Art*, and, *Amazing Grace*, too," she said.

"Oh, you just want, *Amazing Grace*, because it has your name in it," I joked, in a wavering voice. Why? Why couldn't I ever talk about anything serious? Why did I always have to make jokes? Why was I allowing this opportunity to pass me by?

"And, it would be nice to have a pretty blue dress," she said, before I could say something else nonsensical. She wiped her cheeks with her ever—present tissue. Her tears flowed freely now.

Every fiber in my being was screaming, *don't leave me, Mom. I love you so much. I'll miss you more than you'll ever know. I want you to know how much it meant to me as a child to come into the house and hear you whistling. I want you to know how much I loved weekends because you baked bread and pies. I want you to know how much I appreciated the bright red scooter that you bought me for Christmas when we had so little money. I want you to know what it meant to me to have a chance to take piano lessons. I want you to know how much it hurts me to see you suffer. I want you to know how much I love you. Do you think often about dying? Are you afraid to die? Is there anything you want to say to me? I'm so sorry for everything that I did that I shouldn't have done. And I'm sorry for everything that I didn't do that I should've done. I love you, Mom. Don't leave me Mom . . .*

Leaning over the bed, I cradled Mom's withered, skeletal shell against me and rocked her back and forth tenderly. Clamping my quivering lips together to hold back the sobs that were welling inside of me, I allowed the moment to pass. All I could manage was a weak and feeble, barely audible, "I love you, Mom."

Would I ever be able to cope with emotional situations? Would I ever stop being afraid of making myself vulnerable and opening up to people? I mentally berated and whipped myself, but I couldn't seize the opportunity to share my inner—most thoughts and feelings . . . . with anyone.

Right now, I was scared that Mom would die, or that Stephanie would die, or that they both would die, or . . . . and yet I knew I wouldn't share this with anyone, including Ronnie. I felt like I was in the middle of the ocean, in a leaking rowboat, and the wind and waves were spinning the boat in circles, and I was without an oar to paddle, without a bucket to bail out the water. I had no chance to get to shore. Everything was out of control. Everything was out of *my* control.

Now, it was Labor Day, and we were having a family picnic at a park close to the nursing home. Everyone arrived with their food, drinks, and sports equipment. The weather was sunny and unusually hot for September with little or no breeze, perfect for picnicking and playing games. Mom couldn't participate in the games that we played, but she loved watching all of us. Her eyes twinkled in delight as we teased, taunted, and kidded each other. And, at times, she was the object of our teasing.

"I'm your favorite, right Mom?" My brother Gary started his usual routine.

"Gary, don't say that. I don't have any favorites. I love *all* of youse," Mom replied, emphatically, using her Western Pennsylvania vernacular. It was a game with Gary, and it always got the response from Mom that he wanted.

"You know that you love me more, Mom, but you don't want to say it in front of all the others." Gary puffed up his chest and angled his head to one side like a proud peacock.

"Gary, I'm gonna smack you if you don't stop saying those things."

Gary laughed, hugged mom, and wandered off to see who else he could torment.

"Who thinks they can beat me at horseshoes?" He bellowed out his challenge.

Stephanie and George sat next to Gramma, ready to get her a napkin, a drink, another piece of fried chicken, or anything else that she couldn't reach. They would be Gramma's guardians for the day.

I stood looking at the brownies, cookies, and cakes that my sister, Janice, had baked, trying to decide if I should have dessert now or wait until later, when I heard a wheezing, gasping sound.

"What's the matter Mom?" I worked my way through the tables and benches to her side. She was struggling to breathe, and her face was sweaty and gray.

"I can't . . . breathe. I need . . . my thing . . . to squirt. It's in . . . my . . . pock . . ." Her voice trailed off. She was hooked up to her oxygen tank, and small portable fans were aimed directly on her, but it wasn't enough.

Everyone crowded around her. *Are you okay, Mom? Do you need some water? Where's your inhaler? Should we get her to the hospital?* The questions sailed back and forth like a kite in the wind. Everyone was trying to help.

Stephanie's eyes were fastened on her Gramma, and her arms clutched George to her chest. She wasn't sure what was happening, but she knew it wasn't good.

Someone rummaged through Mom's pocketbook and found her medicine. Placing the inhaler in her mouth, she gave herself three rapid spurts of the medicine. We watched her closely. Her head was tilted back against the head restraint on her wheelchair. Still, her breathing was uneven and ragged, and the color didn't come back into her face. She was an ashen-gray.

"Come on, Carole; let's get Mom back to the nursing home." Helen pushed the wheelchair towards the parking lot.

You'll be okay, Mom . . . You just need to get out of the heat . . . You'll feel better when you get into the air-conditioning . . . We love you, Mom . . . I'll see you later tonight . . . Get some rest, Mom . . . The comments of concern and reassurance rained down on us as we positioned Mom in the front seat of the car and stowed her chair in the trunk.

I crushed the gas pedal and sped down the road. The nursing home was only three miles from the park, but I knew by the color of Mom's face that we needed to get her there in a hurry. Her eyes were closed and she was making short gasping sounds, struggling for air.

The doctor on call met us in the hallway. He folded his arms and leaned against the wooden rail that ran along the walls providing support for the residents when they roamed the hallways. With a frown on his face, he explained that Mom was still recovering from her close call. He warned us that we would have to curtail our outings with her. She could no longer function in the heat with the small lung capacity that she had left.

I averted my eyes from his intense stare and watched the clock on the wall behind his shoulder. I was embarrassed. From the tone of his voice and his posture, I knew he thought we should have realized that without being told.

As we walked down the hall to Mom's room, I felt certain that we were one step closer to what I didn't want to face. One step closer to having to explain Mom's absence to Stephanie.

On Wednesday afternoon I hurried home to make an early dinner since it was my day to visit with Mom. I would visit her anyway, but when it was my specified day, I tried to get there earlier and stay later. I was still shaken from the episode at the park, so I was determined to spend as much time with Mom as I could.

"I'll go with you. We can clean up the dishes when we come home." Ronnie grabbed his jacket out of the closet.

"Are you ready Stephanie?" I yelled up the stairway. Gulping down her last bite of food, she had hurried upstairs to get her money so that she could buy a Dr Pepper on the way up to Mom's room.

"I'm ready," she hollered down the stairs, "but George wants to go along, so I have to put his shoes on him." George had spent the day at home, so he was ready to go out and about.

I smiled.

Stephanie was a creature of habit. She needed structure in her life, which allowed her to maintain a comfort level through familiarity, which gave her a sense of security. It scared me to shake up her world, something I'd only had to do occasionally. The last time was when Mom moved to the nursing home. For all of Stephanie's twenty-three years, at least the years that she could remember, Mom lived in the same place by herself. Now I was going to tell her that her grandmother lived in this place that looked a lot like a hospital with many, many other people. There was no question that Stephanie hated hospitals; she related them to pain from shots and the intrusion of probing hands. And, while she loved people, she wouldn't understand the condition in which she was going to see many of these people. I still recall how nervous I was when I tapped on Stephanie's bedroom door that day and peeked inside.

As usual she was sprawled on the floor next to her bed, singing along to a tape of Kenny Rogers's songs. She was holding George's hands, bouncing him up and down on the carpet, making him dance to the music. I turned off the tape player, sat on the edge of her bed, and asked her to sit with me.

"Steph, we had to move Gramma to another house where she'll just have one room with a bed, a chair, and a chest where she'll keep her clothes." She wouldn't understand what a nursing home was. I watched her face as she frowned and studied what I had just said.

"Why did she go there? Doesn't she want to watch TV and cook any more?" A puzzled look played across her face.

I laughed. "Oh, she'll have her TV, but she won't have to cook any more. Isn't that great? It'll be like eating in a restaurant for every meal."

"We can still go see her, can't we?" It appeared that her only concern was maintaining contact with her Gramma. I was relieved.

"Yes, we can still see her. And, you know what? We'll get to see her more often, because she'll be a lot closer to us now." That was easy, I thought. Now we just had to get her used to the other people.

"I'm takin' George 'cause he wants to see Gramma too." It was going to be her first visit to the nursing home.

"That's good. Gramma likes George. She'll be happy to see him." George might be the familiarity and security Stephanie would need when facing the wheelchairs, filled with people in various states of vegetation, lined up on either side of the crowded hallways. George was welcome.

When we entered the front lobby, Stephanie's eyes grew large and her bottom lip quivered. It looked much too much like a hospital. She squeezed my hand as her pace slowed. "It's okay," I said, "Gramma lives on the second floor. We have to take the elevator." She sidled up against my arm, clutching George against her chest, her body stiffening.

As we stepped out of the elevator, I could see the panic in Stephanie's eyes.

"Mommy, Mommy," she cried, as multiple hands stretched out to touch her and George. "No, no, leave me alone," she pleaded, as other feeble hands reached to stroke her. She pressed herself against my side.

"It's okay, honey. They just want to touch you and George. They don't get to see little girls very often." I discreetly moved Stephanie out of their reach.

Kneeling beside Stephanie, I offered my hand to a bird-like, spindly, gray-haired woman, bundled in an old torn afghan. Her trembling, wrinkled hand covered mine. Her watery eyes softened as she smiled gratefully. But her gaze didn't stay on me for long. She was much more interested in Stephanie and George than she was in me. Acknowledging her interest in Stephanie, I said, "Do you like children?" She sat staring at Stephanie. "Do you have grandchildren?" She looked at me briefly, but then returned her attention to Stephanie.

"Honey, would you like to let this woman touch your hand?" Stephanie looked at me warily. "Honey, many of these people don't have visitors like Gramma does, so they get really lonesome." Her eyes fastened on the old woman's hand covering mine. "You know I'd never allow anybody to hurt you, but you don't have to do it if you don't want."

Slowly, she released her grip on George and hesitantly extended her arm towards the woman, resting her hand lightly on top of our joined hands. The old woman's gaze darted in that direction. Then, her thin, pale lips spread in an appreciative smile, revealing a mouthful of yellowed, crooked teeth, as she looked lovingly at Stephanie. And the glow that emanated from her face overshadowed any imperfections brought on by age and illness. Stephanie smiled back.

We said our good-byes and cautiously picked our way through the maze of sad, but hopeful, seeking eyes and desperately searching frail and feeble hands.

That first encounter was only the beginning of many hours of sharing and making friends over the next two years. Stephanie's best friends at the nursing home turned out to be Euffie, the nurses, and the soda machine.

Euffie Gibson didn't always remember what had happened recently, but she could recall most everything that had happened to her years ago. She was in the early stages of Alzheimer's disease. She was an energetic, highly active, petite woman with an infectious personality and a mop of pure white hair, ornery grin and dancing brown eyes. She made friends with Mom and took her under her wing, acting as Mom's hands and feet, getting and delivering what Mom couldn't reach from her bed.

Stephanie liked spending time with Euffie because she made her laugh, she was mobile, and most of the time she could carry on a reasonable conversation, spiced with child-like humor.

The nurses liked Stephanie because she was funny, affectionate, curious, and caring. Stephanie liked the nurses because they always welcomed her and George with warmth and enthusiasm; they were never too busy to stop and talk to her.

And Stephanie's friendship with the soda machine? If they took Dr Pepper out of the machine, the relationship would be over.

Now, two years later, visits to the nursing home were fun and routine. Stephanie had grown comfortable with her Gramma living in the home, and she looked forward to seeing the residents and the nurses.

We arrived just as Mom's tray of food had been delivered, and she was raised in a sitting position. "Oh, we got here just in time for dinner," I teased.

"And I'm hungry." Mom raked her fork through her mashed potatoes, mixing in the gravy.

Being on a steroid to help expand her lungs for the past two years had given Mom a voracious appetite, but recently she had complained that she wasn't hungry and nothing tasted good to her. Now my heart warmed to see her so eager to eat.

"I guess Stephanie stopped to get a Dr Pepper." It was more a statement of fact than a question. Mom stretched her neck, looking out the door into the hallway. "She'd better get here soon. I feel like playing." She smiled like someone who couldn't wait to share a secret.

I watched as she chopped her meatloaf into bite-sized pieces and slathered butter over her peas and her dinner roll.

"So, do you think it's nice to eat in front of us? I haven't had my dinner yet," Ronnie joked. He moved to the side of her bed and sniffed, pretending to savor the smell of her meal.

Steadying her glass with both hands and guiding it to her mouth, Mom laughed and took a drink of her iced tea.

By the time she was finished eating, Stephanie had arrived with her Dr Pepper. "I'll bet you can't say this rhyme without making a mistake," Mom challenged Stephanie. *"She sells seashells, down by the seashore . . ."* They giggled and clapped their hands each time one of them messed up.

I sat on the empty bed next to the window, smiling, laughing and enjoying watching them play with each other. Mom's roommate had died recently and they hadn't filled the bed as yet. It was nice having the room all to ourselves.

"Okay, let's do *"Hey, diddle, diddle."* Mom popped a cough drop into her mouth. They recited together: *"Hey, diddle, diddle, the cat and the fiddle, the cow jumped over the moon. The little dog laughed to see such sport, and the dish ran away with the spoon."* Mom grabbed the spoon from her tray and waved it in the air, and then pulled Stephanie against her and kissed her on the top of her head. They laughed, celebrating their success.

Ronnie, sitting in the burgundy vinyl armchair next to Mom's bed, looked up from the magazine he was reading and laughed with them.

"Okay, now sing a song with me." Mom closed her eyes for a moment, sighed, and smiled at Stephanie.

"Jesus loves me, this I know, for the bible tells me so . . ." Stephanie stood leaning against the bed, holding Mom's hand and cradling George in her other arm. Her voice squeaked, trying to reach the high notes, and their voices drowned out the noise of TV programs filtering in from other rooms. Mom dropped her box of cough drops into her lap and covered their clasped hands with her free hand.

The rhythm of my heart changed. I moved to the side of the bed.

"I'm so glad that youse *all* came tonight. It felt good to laugh so much." Mom hugged Stephanie and gave her a cough drop; then she pulled my head down and kissed me on the cheek. "You know I love youse all." She reached over and squeezed Ronnie's hand. I could feel the tears welling in my eyes. I straightened and kissed the sparse, gray hair on her head.

Don't cry. Don't cry.

The next morning, I placed the hair dryer back in the rack and gave my hair one last swish with the brush just as the phone rang. Who would be calling us six-thirty in the morning?

Seconds later, Ronnie walked into the bathroom carrying the phone. One look at him and my heart began to pound. I could feel the color draining from my face.

"It's Rick. Your mom passed away this morning."

With a trembling hand, I reached for the phone. How could I not be prepared for this? Tears burned my eyes. "Rick?" I squeaked. "When?"

"Just a few minutes ago. She was having trouble breathing. The nurse left the room to get her medicine and when she got back Mom was gone." My brother's voice sounded tired and resigned.

"I'll see you at the nursing home." I offered no comfort. I was numb.

I hesitated at the door. Mom's head, with her mouth open, was tilted back on the pillow. If I hadn't received the phone call from Rick, I would have thought she was sleeping. Occasionally, when we arrived to visit her, Mom would be in this same position taking a nap. We would sit quietly waiting for her to wake up.

"She looked so good last night. She ate all of her dinner. She laughed and joked. Her voice was strong. Ronnie and I talked about how she seemed to be so much better than she'd been in a while." I babbled on, hugging each sister and brother.

"She does look peaceful," Lorraine said, stroking Mom's brow.

We clung to each other, crying, mumbling words of consolation and assurance.

"I guess there's no need to have these fans running now." Janice reached for the switch on the fan next to the head of Mom's bed.

"Don't turn that off," I shouted at Janice and hurried around the side of the bed towards the fan. All eyes were on me. The only sound in the room was the whirring of the fan blades. Janice withdrew her hand.

"I'm sorry. It's just that Mom can't breathe without the fans. Please . . . don't . . ."

Deciding that it would be best to tell Stephanie about Mom in a place where she was the most comfortable and felt the most secure, I took her to her bedroom. George was in his bassinet taking his afternoon nap, so neither Kenny Rogers nor Anne Murray was performing. I would have her full attention.

I took off my shoes and climbed up on the bed, pulling her along with me. I propped the pillows behind my head and snuggled her against my chest.

"Stephie, I have to talk to you about Gramma." I began by explaining that we wouldn't be going to the nursing home or to the hospital anymore to see Gramma because she wouldn't be there. We wouldn't see her ever again.

"Why doesn't Gramma want to see us again?" It had never occurred to me that she would think Gramma didn't want to see *us*.

"No, honey, it's not that Gramma doesn't want to see us. She loves us."

I searched my mind trying to remember the death of one of their pets that would help explain what I was trying to tell her. I reminded her of Gourd, Robyn's cat, and how he got old and sick and died. Stephanie's puzzled look turned into gradual understanding.

"Well, in a way, that's what happened to Gramma. She's been sick for a long time, and her body just got too tired to keep on going, so Gramma is going to heaven to rest." Stephanie knew about heaven from Sunday school.

Tears trickled down her face. "But I won't be able to talk to her."

"Oh, yes you will." I hugged her close. "Maybe you won't be able to hear Gramma answer you, but she'll be in heaven listening to anything and everything that you want to say to her. You just look up and talk to her any time you want."

"Okay. Okay!" She squirmed out of my arms and slid off the bed, dancing and giggling nervously. Pointing her tiny, crooked finger upward, she instructed, "Gramma, you better behave up there. Do you hear me?" She bounced back up onto the bed and held my face with her hands. "Mommy, can I go up to see her sometime?" Her voice screeched in excitement.

Later, as I prepared dinner, I couldn't forget what Stephanie had said. '. . . *Can I go up to see her sometime?*' With each beat of my heart, her words pulsed through my body. '. . . *Can I go up to see her sometime?*' With each step that I took, her words shadowed me. '. . . *Can I go up to see her sometime?*' Her words wrapped me in a cocoon of fear and trepidation.

I steer my bark with hope in my heart,
Leaving fear astern.

Thomas Jefferson

When I walked into the living room, I knew something was wrong. Stephanie wasn't hiding from me and Ronnie wasn't reading his newspaper. My heart began to race. "Where's Stephanie?" Ronnie was standing by the fireplace, his hands jammed in his pants pockets, his face an indisputable mask of concern.

"Don't get upset. She's okay, but she had another seizure today." He walked towards me. "She's upstairs resting."

I ran past him, flew up the stairs and raced into her bedroom. Stephanie never rested. It must be bad.

She was asleep. I crept onto the bed and cradled her in my arms.

It had been a grand mal seizure. Again, there were bumps and bruises but, fortunately, she fell in the hallway at the college, and she wasn't near any steps. Ronnie and I agreed that she would have to stay with him at all times. She could visit with her friends when Ronnie was free to go with her, but there would be no more going from one room to another without him.

Now every day at school was even more stressful. I continually watched the clock, called Ronnie's office in between classes, and hurried home as soon as I could complete my responsibilities.

I had plenty of sick leave and personal leave days, but something told me to hang onto them until I really needed them.

They wanted to do the MRI without sedation, but when they told Stephanie that she would have to be perfectly still, it only made her move more. She had always had a slight jerk and twitch to her head, and when she was trying to concentrate it became more exaggerated.

Sedation was the only way. I held her hand and stroked her arm while the medication was taking hold. Then I retreated to a chair close by as they slid her into the thumping, tomb-like apparatus. If only I could take away her fear. If only I could take away her pain. If only I could take her place. If . . . If . . . If . . . I felt the world closing in on me as though I were the one being put into the oppressive, suffocating passage.

Shortly after we arrived home Stephanie sat on the family room floor working her latest puzzle, while George sat on the floor next to her. The phone rang. It was the neurologist from the hospital. "I've just read Stephanie's MRI and . . ." He paused and cleared his throat. "The results are a bit confusing."

My heart was pounding. "Why?" I dashed up the steps to the kitchen. This wasn't good news, and I didn't want Stephanie to see the panic on my face.

"There is definitely something showing on the MRI, and, quite frankly, it's like nothing that I've ever seen before." Again he paused. "I just don't feel qualified to deal with it. I think you need to arrange an appointment with a neurologist that works out of a larger hospital as soon as possible."

"What are you saying? Is it a tumor? What do you mean when you say it's nothing like you've ever seen before?" I couldn't breathe. Why was he telling me this over the phone? Why weren't we sitting down together and going over the MRI? What was Ronnie thinking, sitting downstairs in the family room with Stephanie? Surely he could hear the panic in my voice. I wrapped my arms around myself, clutched the phone to my ear, and huddled in the corner next to the dry sink at the top of the stairs.

"Yes, I would say it's a tumor, but it's shaped differently than other tumors that I've seen."

I couldn't respond. I was devastated. I had been fairly certain that the seizures were a result of a problem other than her retardation, but a brain tumor? Maybe I had even suspected a tumor, but it was overwhelming to hear a doctor say it.

"Did you hear me?"

"Yes, I heard you," I murmured.

I took several deep breaths, pursed my lips to keep them from quivering, and walked back down to the family room. "That was the neurologist. He wants us to see another doctor . . . soon." I was choosing my words carefully so that Ronnie would get the message, but Stephanie wouldn't pick up on the urgency.

Ronnie did get the message. He gathered Stephanie into his arms, rocking her back and forth, stroking her back, and nuzzling his face in her hair. When he raised his head, he looked at me, pleadingly, as if to say, *make it all go away*.

A few minutes later, upstairs again, I grabbed the phone and called Helen, my older sister, the one I turned to when I felt overwhelmed and wasn't sure what to do next.

No answer.

I called my sister Janice.

"Is your mom around?" I asked my niece, Stacy, when she answered the phone. I could feel myself losing control. My voice quavered.

"No, she and dad are out. Aunt Carole what's wrong?"

"It's Stephanie. I . . . it's bad news . . . . the results of her MRI . . . .", my voice trailed off. I couldn't continue.

"Aunt Carole, hang up. I'll find mom. I'll have her call you back."

' . . . Can I go up to see her sometime?' I hurried into the bathroom and, crouched in the corner, wept tears of anguish.

Sleep was impossible. I tossed and turned. My mind raced from one scenario to another. Could I possibly lose my child so soon after just losing my mother? And, then, I began to talk to myself, demanding that I think rationally. After all, the neurologist didn't say anything that should lead us to believe that Steph's condition was hopeless. And besides, he didn't even recognize what kind of tumor it was. He simply said he wasn't qualified to deal with what he saw. I would remain calm, I would go about my daily routine, and I would be the eternal optimist that I had always been.

But, as I tossed and turned, stared at the ceiling, and willed myself to go to sleep, I recalled the words that Dr. James had said to me many years ago. *"Mother's have an innate sense when it comes to raising their children. There's a bond, or a connection, if you will, that helps mothers know when all is not well."*

All was not well, and I didn't want to know why.

The trip for our appointment with Dr. Turner, the neurologist in Baltimore, scheduled for the following Wednesday morning, was uneventful, but interspersed with the usual questions and comments. *But, why do I hafta go to the doctor? . . . I feel okay . . . . Dr. Thompson put me on medicine . . . . Who is this doctor anyway? . . . . What is he gonna do to me? . . . . He'd better not give me a shot . . . . If George doesn't like him, he'll probably punch him in the nose . . . . Why do I always have to go to the doctor?*

It was a question I had asked myself over the years. Why Stephanie?

After many trips to the orthopedic hospital, and two years in her brace, Stephanie was walking. She waddled slightly, and couldn't run fast, but she was mobile.

But, not long after she started walking, our enthusiasm over the success of the brace was diminished when we learned that Stephanie had a 45% hearing loss in both ears, and she'd need two hearing aids. We had noticed that she didn't appear to be hearing us unless she was facing us. The audiologist explained that she'd been compensating for her hearing loss by reading our lips.

After getting her hearing aids, we noticed that Stephanie still sat too close to the TV, so our next trip was to the optometrist. The stems on her glasses would be shaped to fit comfortably behind her hearing aids.

Through the weeks and months that followed, with many visits for adjustments, Stephanie became accustomed to the nuances of taking care of and wearing her hearing aids and glasses.

We had spent so much time concentrating on Stephanie's quest to walk, hear and see that we had unintentionally neglected her academic skills. While we read to her, showed her picture books of animals, fruits, vegetables, numbers and colors, gave her crayons, pencils, scissors, coloring books and paper, exposed her to outside activities with playmates, animals, and her sister Robyn, we hadn't had her tested to get an official reading of her mental aptitudes.

Though Stephanie played well with other children, she preferred animals. She liked dogs and rabbits, but cats were her favorite. She trained her cats to behave the way she wanted them to. She dressed them, fed them by hand, pushed them around in a baby stroller, tucked them into a slip-shod bed made from pieces of scrap wood, cloth remnants, and dried cornstalks, and reprimanded them when they were naughty.

One day we found Stephanie sitting on the steps to the back porch eating out of the same pan that her kitten, Jangles, and her rabbit, Midnight, were sharing. Picking up the small brown nuggets, she was saying, *One for you, one for me.* In Stephanie's mind, if the food was good enough for Jangles and Midnight, it certainly was good enough for her.

From the time she was five years old, Stephanie spent many hours at the ball field as the mascot to my Little League teams. The girls, ages 9 through 12, encouraged and praised Stephanie as her skinny little legs wobbled as she hurried to pick up the bats that the girls dropped at home plate after they hit the ball. She carefully placed the bats in the bat rack, made her way through the dugout, and continued to cheer, repeating the phrases that she heard every day.

Hit the ball . . . get a 'tweener . . . .. run, run, run . . . .. foul ball . . . . fair ball . . . . way to go . . . you can do it . . . get your glove down on the ground . . . atta girl . . . .. atta girl.

She loved being a part of the team. She also loved the hot dogs, Dr Peppers, and the attention that all of the girls, and their parents, showered upon her.

Ronnie attended all of the games, watching Robyn pitch and taking care of anything that Stephanie might need while I was coaching.

But, as much as she was exposed to, and as much as we tried to teach her at home, we knew she had to be tested and placed into the appropriate classroom setting, so in early June, a month before her sixth birthday, we took her to a doctor who specialized in testing and evaluating mentally retarded children. Though she worked out of Baltimore, she agreed to meet with us in a county office building close to our home.

We weren't allowed to go into the room with Stephanie, so she cried and clung to my leg, but when they promised her that she could color, draw, and play some games, and I promised I would be sitting outside of the door waiting for her, she reluctantly released her grip on my leg and followed the doctor into a small room with short-legged tables and chairs.

An hour-and-a-half later, we sat facing Dr. Patterson. She sat at the desk scratching out a few more notes on her stack of papers. We waited silently. She raised her head. "According to the Stanford-Binet Intelligence Scale and the Merrill-Palmer Scale of Mental Tests, Stephanie's IQ is approximately 55. She is what we refer to as TMR, or trainable, mentally retarded. Do you have any questions?" She dropped her pen on top of the papers and folded her arms, her shrill and abrasive voice stripping me of any fragment of hope. Her brusque and aloof recitation trampled the delicate, fragile defense that I had managed to cower beneath. I fastened my eyes on the stack of papers.

Ronnie shifted in his chair and cleared his throat. "I guess one question that we have concerns her schooling." He uncrossed his legs and stood up, nervously moving behind his chair. "Will she be able to function in a regular classroom with help, or will she have to attend a school specifically for mentally retarded students?"

When the doctor hesitated, I took a deep breath, trying to purge my body of the hostility and outrage that her attitude had released in me. "What should we expect Stephanie to be able to accomplish down the road?" I fought to keep my voice from shaking.

Doctor Patterson leaned back in her chair, sighed heavily and responded, "I'm not sure how to answer your first question because I'm not really familiar with your school system, but the answer to your second question . . ." She paused, sat up straight, tapped the stack of papers, placed her elbows on the desk and said, "Someday she might be able to ride a bus alone."

I could feel the blood draining from my face. I could feel my heart racing. I could feel that sliver of hope dissipating.

We sat immobilized.

"Well, if you have no other questions, I'll see that you get a copy of my report." She glanced at her wristwatch. "I have another appointment in Baltimore." She stood up, stuffed the papers into her briefcase, and disappeared through the door.

We sat immobilized.

She had come to Cecil County, twisted and turned the stake that already penetrated our hearts, and hurried back to Baltimore.

Neither of us had the energy nor the desire to talk on the way home. What more was there to say?

Robyn knew that we had an appointment with a doctor who could tell us what to expect from and for Stephanie in the future. At least that's how I had explained it to her. So, when she hurried in from school, I knew she'd ask questions. I really wasn't prepared to discuss what had happened at our meeting, just yet, so I deliberately busied myself and avoided eye contact with her.

Finally, it was time to get dressed in our uniforms for the softball game. Now, I thought, Robyn will be caught up in the excitement of the game, since she was pitching, and she'll forget to ask me. I needed time to formulate an answer that would not overwhelm her as we had been overwhelmed.

We climbed in the car with Stephanie seated between us. I could feel Robyn's eyes fixed on me. I stared straight ahead. "So, what did the doctor say today?"

I took a deep breath. I considered not telling her the truth, but I knew I would have to tell her someday. "Stephanie will have to have someone look after her for all of her life."

Did I say the right thing? At the age of eleven would she understand what that meant?

Robyn turned in her seat, slid her arm around Stephanie's shoulders, pulling her delicate frame up against her own scrawny body. I knew if I squeezed my eyes any tighter, I wouldn't be able to see to drive. I was stifling tears of pride and pain.

A week later, I sat at the kitchen table willing myself to pick up the large yellow envelope, with the Baltimore address, that had arrived in the morning mail. I walked to the stove and heated some water for a cup of tea. I glanced at the envelope. I dipped the tea bag up and down, slowly and deliberately, into the cup of hot water. I glanced at the envelope. I wrapped the tea bag around the spoon and drained every drop of the mint flavored water into the cup. I glanced at the envelope. I added sugar to the tea.

Finally, I picked up the envelope and ripped it open.

I sat staring at the unusually large print. I discarded the cover letter and scanned the sheet headed: *CONFIDENTIAL*, then let my eyes slide down to the section identified as *Test Results*.

Though I had prepped myself to accept and cope with the reading of her low scores and the interpretation of the test results, I wasn't prepared for the debilitating shock and the piercing sting that spread through me when I read the actual words of the official report.

I.Q 55 . . . . scores on the Stanford-Binet place her at the high moderately retarded level . . . has few visible academic skills . . . The paper shook in my hand . . . *found to be functioning within the moderately mentally retarded range . . .* My chest tightened . . . *pleasant, friendly and cooperative youngster . . . . eager to please . . . . appealing . . . petite and almost fragile in appearance . . .* My heart ached with pride . . . *speaks clearly . . . content of her verbalizations is limited . . . easily distracted . . . both fine and gross motor coordination are immature for age . . . would be most appropriately placed in a trainable class . . .*

A deep, despairing sadness settled over me.

Her *problems* were now substantiated facts. Her *problems* were now documented on letterhead paper. Her *problems* now had numbers and names.

While I dealt with the implications of Stephanie's test results privately and without question, Ronnie wasn't nearly as compliant. He wanted to have Stephanie tested by the Department of Health and Mental Hygiene's Diagnostic and Advisory Service. He wasn't convinced that the test results gave a true picture of Stephanie's capabilities.

I felt that he was grasping at straws but, secretly, I hoped that he was right. His doubt was giving me renewed hope. We set up an appointment for the second test. When the brown manila envelope arrived, I left it on the kitchen table, unopened, waiting for Ronnie to come home. He had wanted the second test done, so I would let him be the first to read it. Besides, I already knew what the report would say, despite the thread of hope that I was clinging to; it would be the same as the first one, and I had no desire to reinforce what I already knew. Reading it would make it more real. It would make it more final. It would render me more helpless.

That afternoon, Ronnie sat at the table reading the official report, his face clouded over with a mixture of pain and frustration.

"This reads exactly like the first one." The disgust in his voice made it clear that he wasn't convinced that either of the reports was accurate. He shuffled the pages, flipping them one at a time back onto the table. "IQ 55." He cast the words into the air like they were polluting his mouth. Picking up the papers he scanned them again, searching for particular statements. Then with a smirk in his voice, he read, *". . . high moderately retarded level . . . pleasant . . . cooperative . . . . petite . . . recommend placement in a trainable class . . ."*

By the time he finished reading, there was more pain than anger in his voice. He slumped in his chair and stared at the floor.

"They obviously have a standard form and then they select their words from a pre-determined package of adjectives and verbs." He jumped up from his chair and opened the refrigerator door, his agitation drifted along behind him. With his soda in his hand, he snarled, "A rubber stamp. One size fits all." He slammed the refrigerator door and stomped out of the kitchen.

Like me, he had clung to a sliver of hope, and now we both had to reconcile ourselves to the irrefutable truth and move on. But, Ronnie was still reluctant to put her into a school for mentally-retarded children, so we continued to teach her at home.

And then, shortly after Stephanie's seventh birthday, Ronnie was approached by a friend who had a handicapped child. He told Ronnie about a program that he and his wife had investigated and were now a part of out of Philadelphia.

They were taking their son to a place called The Institutes for the Achievement of Human Potential. The program, as they explained it to us, was developed in the late 1950s by Dr. Glenn Doman, a physiologist; Dr. Carl Delacato, a psychologist; Dr. Robert Doman Sr., a medical doctor; and Florence Scott, Robert's registered nurse. It was known as the Doman-Delacato Method. This method was the reorganizing of the brain through neurodevelopment. We had no idea what that meant, but we purchased several of Dr. Doman's books and began to familiarize ourselves with the theory.

As we read the books and talked to our friend and his wife, we learned that the one thing that most everybody identified with the program was *patterning*. The child was placed on his or her stomach on a flat surface with an adult positioned at the child's head, and an adult on each side of the child. In a rhythmic pattern, the adults would manipulate the head and arms and legs of the child simulating a crawling motion.

We decided to investigate further and made an appointment to have a consultation with the staff. Armed with questions, copies of several of Doman and Delacato's books, and hearts full of hope, we traveled to Philadelphia.

As we sat in a large room, waiting for our appointed time, I was aghast at what I saw. There were children without appendages. There were children lying on the floor, drooling and moaning. There were children who were blind. There were children with deformed heads. There were children with distorted faces. There were children rocking and squealing. There were children attached to oxygen machines. There were children curled up in a ball on their mother's lap.

And there were parents who were anxiously clinging to yet one more hope, The Institute for the Achievement of Human Potential.

I struck up conversations with several of the parents. They had come from many states and many countries. They all looked tired and nervous. They all looked expectant. They all looked guardedly optimistic.

They recounted their many trials, many travels, and many hopes that all ended in disappointment. Would this trip end in disillusionment also, they wondered?

I was ashamed. There were times when I felt sorry for myself and I asked, *Why me? Why us? Why Stephanie?* Now, I felt guilty for even one such thought when I observed the other children. How could I possibly have ever been so selfish? I should have been counting my blessings for all the joy that Stephanie had brought into our lives.

Dr. Doman and his associates met with us after Stephanie's initial evaluation and gave us a brief overview of what the program entailed and how it would be carried out. Stephanie and I would return to the Institutes for a week of intensive evaluation and training. Because the evaluations and the training began at the crack of dawn and continued on throughout the evening hours, we would have to stay at a motel close to the Institutes.

The decision to go ahead with the program was not an easy one. I would be away from the children for a week. When Stephanie and I came home, our lifestyle would change drastically with the invasion of a series of physical and academic programs and the people needed to carry them out. We would open our doors to our helpers at 8 o'clock in the morning and the parade of people would continue until 8 o'clock at night, and if we stuck with the program, it would cover at least two years of our lives. We had already spent many hours, days, weeks, and years concentrating on Stephanie's needs, but the required doctors' visits, the testing, were all issues that took place *outside* of our home. Now, we would be bringing this intense, time—consuming program *into* our home, invading our privacy and eroding our time together. Was it fair to Robyn, who was going into the sixth grade, and to Jennifer, who had turned a year old just four months ago?

Stephanie needed the extra attention to improve her fine and gross motor coordination and develop her academic skills, but would Robyn and Jennifer understand why we were doing this? Would they grow up resenting her for it?

We talked about it. We weighed both sides. We made our decision. We wavered. We considered. We reconsidered. Finally, we decided.

We owed it to Stephanie. She was already seven years old. We needed to give her every opportunity to progress and develop. I prayed that Robyn and Jennifer would understand some day.

The evaluations were thorough and the training was intense. We, the parents, formed teams and practiced patterning on our children. The children all had their own unique methods, but they all resisted us. Stephanie cried and stiffened her arms and legs, making it difficult to simulate the crawling pattern, but as the week wore on, she, and the other children, tired and gave in to our efforts.

And, though we didn't completely understand the medical reasoning behind the recreating of the crawling motion with our children, we knew it was an important part of the program, so we persisted.

As a team, we learned how to perform numerous other physical activities that were designed to improve fine and gross motor skills, and we learned and practiced many varied methods of stimulating our children intellectually. The most challenging part of the program designed for intellectual stimulus was keeping the kids' attention for any length of time, but we persevered. When we returned to our motel rooms, we, and the children, were exhausted, but it felt good to be working on something positive, something that might possibly be helpful.

After a week of concentrated training and missing every one, Stephanie and I were physically drained and happy to be home. Now the real work would begin.

For two years, with the help of many generous people, we: patterned; did overhead exercises on a monkey bar that Ronnie built; hung Stephanie upside-down from those same bars with straps attached to her feet fastening her to the bars; worked with balls, rubber toys, coins, books, paper and pencils, rulers, scissors, number and letter cards. We performed numerous other physical and academic activities; all geared to help Stephanie improve her fine and gross motor skills and her academic skills.

In the beginning, though Stephanie knew most of her helpers, she resisted them as vigorously as she had me and the team at the Institute, but as the days and weeks wore on she cooperated more frequently and with less bribery. Our grocery bill for cookies, lollipops, chewing gum and Dr Peppers decreased accordingly.

And when she learned to feed off the praise (instead of junk food) of her helpers, she worked harder and harder trying to please them.

During the day, Stephanie got few breaks and mine were fewer. While we had many volunteers, it was seldom that we had a day that I didn't have to participate in the patterning and various other procedures. In addition, I managed to do the housework (albeit in a skimmed-over fashion), the laundry, the grocery shopping, prepare the meals, take care of Robyn and Jennifer, and maintain some semblance of order in our daily lives.

Ronnie helped in the evenings when he had free time, but he was taking classes at Johns Hopkins University, so his time was at a premium. He already had his master's degree from Columbia University, but now, after teaching vocal music throughout his career, he was moving from all music to some education classes at the college. He was spurred on, partly, by what we were experiencing because of Stephanie's mental retardation. He wanted to learn more and so he was getting a second master's degree. Life couldn't get much more hectic.

There were mornings that I wanted to get Ronnie and Robyn off to school, take care of Jennifer and Stephanie's needs, keep all the doors locked, and hide from all of the kind and generous people who, unintentionally, were depleting all of my energy. I wanted to walk away from the program that was stifling me and my family.

There were mornings when I didn't even want to do all of that. I just wanted to stay in bed.

But, when summer arrived, I refused to give up coaching softball, so I adjusted our schedule to allow for practice and games. Four days a week we stopped the program at three-thirty in the afternoon. The break was good for all of us. Jennifer was out in the fresh air, being tracked by her father as she wandered aimlessly around the bleachers, Stephanie was interacting with the girls and their parents, and Robyn was playing ball. And as a family, we were doing something that wasn't focused entirely on Stephanie.

Stephanie and I returned to the Institutes periodically for evaluations and new strategies and, as the days, weeks, months, and finally years went on, Stephanie did show improvement. Her balance was noticeably better, her gait more even, her handwriting steadier. She was identifying coins, determining how many pennies it took to equal a nickel how many nickels it took to equal a dime and how many different coins she could use to add up to a quarter. She was adding numbers, she was reading words from her books, and she was spelling more difficult words.

However, as is human nature, the helpers, for a variety of reasons began to dwindle in number. Of course, there were the staunch supporters who never failed to show up, but it was getting more difficult to enlist replacements for those who couldn't make their appointed times. I couldn't and wouldn't complain. I would be eternally grateful for all that everyone had done.

In addition to the lack of helpers, it was obvious that, as a family, we needed a break. It was time to move on. Although Stephanie had improved, she appeared to have reached a plateau. Jennifer was clearly living in the shadows of what had become a daily display of continual, overabundant attention on Stephanie. As a result of this extreme attention to Stephanie, I worried that Jennifer might be suffering from emotional neglect.

At the age of three-and-a-half, she was much too young to understand Stephanie's many special needs. Robyn came home from school to a procession of adults moving through our house. How could she not resent the hubbub that greeted her return from school each day? After all, she was a teenager now. And Ronnie and I were like ships that passed in the night. We each had our schedules to maintain, and seldom did they coincide.

The neurologist, Dr. Turner, reminded me of Mr. Rogers from the PBS TV program, MR. ROGERS' NEIGHBORHOOD. He looked comfortable and welcoming in his cardigan sweater, his scuffed shoes, and his disarming smile. He greeted us warmly, as if he had known us for a long time. With a wave of his hand, he motioned us to the chairs across from his desk. "Stephanie, I'd like to ask you a few questions."

Though there was a separate chair for Stephanie, she was scrunched into a chair with me. She wasn't about to leave my side in a doctor's office, especially when she had just met him. She twisted her body, cocked her head to one side, and sighed. Her sigh seemed to say, *here we go again.*

After a brief conversation with Stephanie, asking her about any pain, weakness, or dizzy spells that she might have been experiencing, Dr. Turner addressed us in a quiet, but serious tone. "I've seen the MRI from the other hospital. It does show an abnormality in Stephanie's brain." He leaned forward in his chair. "At this point, I'm not ready to identify exactly what that abnormality is." He paused and looked at Stephanie. Was she listening? "I do feel a certain urgency to begin testing." His smile had disappeared.

We spent the rest of the day shuffling from one area of the hospital to another, waiting in between the tests, talking to various doctors and technicians. Dr. Turner, we were told, would be in touch with us.

By now it was dark and we were catching the tail-end of the rush—hour traffic.

"Mommy, Mommy, it's startin again!"

"Pull over, Ronnie," I shouted. In the back seat of the car, Stephanie's fatigued, frail body was contorting and flailing. Scrambling into the back seat, I held her while the seizure ran its course. Finally, her body relaxed against me. She wept softly.

"Mommy, I knew it was gonna happen. I could feel it crawlin up my leg." She clung to me, afraid to let go, afraid it would crawl up her leg again.

"Which leg, honey?"

"This one." She placed her hand on her left knee.

"Does it hurt?" Instinctively, I began rubbing her leg.

"It feels tired and my foot hurts."

For the rest of the ride home, I cradled her in my arms and gently stroked her tiny forehead, while she cuddled George. While Ronnie concentrated on the road, I sat holding Stephanie, wondering what the future held for us. Based on our past, I was sure that the future would be anything but ordinary.

Now that Stephanie was no longer involved in a structured program, we knew we needed to start her education in a regular school setting, and though the recommendations had been that Stephanie be placed in a *trainable class*, Ronnie wanted to put her into a regular first grade class, with resource room help. The school system complied, stipulating that her progress and ability to cope, both academically and emotionally, should be monitored carefully.

It wasn't long, however, before it was obvious that her comprehension skills weren't sufficient to keep pace with the other first graders. Though she could read and write, somewhat, she wasn't nearly as proficient as the others in the class.

We were alerted that, at the end of the first semester, she would be moved from the regular classroom into a trainable class.

Ronnie was teaching education classes at the local community college and, in one class, he had several wonderfully kind nuns who suggested that maybe Stephanie would do well in their private Catholic school. Ronnie wanted to try it.

Stephanie thrived under the nuns' tutelage and loving care, but, after a year, they decided that they, and their school, weren't equipped to take somebody with Stephanie's limitations any further in the classroom. We said a tearful goodbye to the nuns and put her into the public school's special wing for retarded and handicapped children.

While Ronnie struggled with her placement, I was relieved that Stephanie would be in a classroom where she could feel successful and comfortable. At the age of nine, she would finally feel that she belonged.

Our local elementary school didn't have a program for special-needs children, so Stephanie attended a school in a town 15 miles away. This, of course, meant a long and tedious bus ride, not only because of the distance to the school, but because the buses available for the *special* kids were limited and had to cover a large area.

One day I returned home from school, and Ronnie was pacing the floor, his face flushed with anger. "They dropped Stephanie off at the wrong bus stop."

My heart lurched.

"She's here. Don't panic."

He explained that the substitute bus driver had dropped Stephanie off at a trailer park, and a mother of another child, recognizing that Stephanie didn't belong there, called Ronnie and he had picked her up.

I ran up the stairs and pushed open the door. She was sprawled on the floor dressing George and listening to her tapes. I sat down on the floor beside her and hugged her close. "What happened today? Why did you get off the bus at the trailer park?" She knew where she lived. She wouldn't get off the bus at the wrong place without a good reason.

"The bus driver told me to get off. She wouldn't listen to me. I knew it was the wrong place." She continued dressing George.

"Were you scared? What did you do?"

"Yeah, I was scared, but the lady asked me my name and my father's name. I told her and she called daddy." She smiled and pulled George's pants up over his diaper.

To Stephanie, it was just another day. To me, it was one more setback in her young, but troubled, life. We would not only have to watch over Stephanie, but we would have to watch over those who were, supposedly, watching over her. What if the nice woman hadn't noticed Stephanie getting off the bus? What if someone else, not so nice, had noticed Stephanie?

For weeks, I called home from school about the time Stephanie's bus should have delivered her, making sure that she was with Ronnie, checking to make sure that there wasn't another mistake made. Gradually, I relaxed, but ensuring her safety was never out of my mind.

Stephanie blossomed at the school for handicapped children. She could already read and write on a nominal basis, but with the concentrated attention that she received at the school, she was reading more fluently, reciting her ABCs, understanding the concept of less and more, and improving her ability to verbalize what she understood but had always struggled to put into words.

Quickly, she became a leader and a helper. After finishing her work, she would go to the desks of the less proficient students who were struggling and help with the control of a pencil, the ordering of letters, and the sequence of numbers. She reminded the kids that they should walk in a straight line when going to the lunch room and stay in line while waiting for the bus. She admonished the kids who didn't clean up their mess in the lunch room or straighten the materials on their desks.

She was a mini-version of me. She followed the rules and regulations and, if others didn't, it distressed her mightily. After all, why did we have rules and regulations if we weren't supposed to abide by them?

Her nurturing instincts, which she had honed on her many dolls and animals, became more obvious as she aided the teachers when catastrophe struck. If one of the students got upset and created a scene, slowing down the operation of the class, she sat with them, soothing and calming them; if someone got hurt, she pacified them and assured them that everything would be okay. Often she would repeat what she heard my assistant softball coach say many times during practice and games when one of the girls suffered a minor injury. *It'll be better before you get married.*

And she loved socializing. One afternoon, after school, as I walked in the door, she came bounding into the kitchen.

"Mommy, we're having a party next week. Can you come?" She plopped her lunch box and a handful of papers on the table.

"What kind of party?" I shuffled through the papers, looking for an invitation from her teacher.

She opened her lunch box and produced a homemade invitation. "Here Mommy, you can read it." She thrust it into my hand.

I knew it was special if she transported it inside of her lunch box instead of in her hand with all of her other papers.

In bright red crayon, she had scrawled:

> *Come to our party—Mothers only!*
> *At 12 o'clock on May sixth*
> *For lunch and special entertainment*

"Wow," I exclaimed, "Special entertainment? What are *you* going to do?"

"I'm not allowed to tell. My teacher said it's our secret. If you wanna know, you'll hafta come."

I made a mental note to request a day off from school.

The morning of the party, Stephanie bounced out of bed, rushed into my bedroom and tugged on the covers. Her face was glowing with excitement. "Mommy, it's party day." She climbed up on the bed and sat on me. "You gotta get up. I can't be late. There's a lot I hafta do to get ready."

At the breakfast table, she giggled and fidgeted in between spoonfuls of *Lucky Charms*. "You just wait. You'll be surprised." She wriggled off her chair and plopped onto my lap, clapping her hands. "You're never gonna guess what we're gonna do." It was all she could do to keep *her secret.*

I had met her teacher and the principal of the school at Stephanie's Individual Education Program (IEP) meeting. Today I would meet the other teachers and the aides. Between the anticipation of meeting everyone who worked with Stephanie and finding out what the special entertainment was, I was almost as excited as she was.

As the mothers entered the building, we were greeted by our *special* student and led to the cafeteria where we would be fed and entertained.

The rectangular tables, surrounded by metal folding chairs, were placed in two long rows, leaving just enough room for the students to maneuver as they carried our plates of breaded chicken breasts, rice, and corn. Baskets of rolls and pats of butter were already on the tables.

The tiled walls were adorned with student drawings and paintings on different colored construction paper.

The children were enthusiastic and animated as they scurried back and forth bringing us our beverages. What did we want? Water? A soft drink? Iced tea? Liquids splashed from container to tray but, eventually, we all had our somewhat less—than—full glasses.

Through all the hustle and bustle, it was clear that the students weren't as interested in eating as they were in getting to the special entertainment. Quickly, they cleared, wiped, and removed the tables, placed the chairs into a semi-circle, and directed us to sit. Then they exited the cafeteria.

The principal welcomed us to the party, made a few remarks commending the teachers and the students for doing a fine job preparing the Mother's Day luncheon and the entertainment, and then signaled to the teachers who were waiting at one of the entrances.

The students came marching in, dressed in an assortment of sparkle-laden homemade costumes, and playing a collection of rhythm instruments. Stephanie was banging two sticks together and beaming at me. There was bedlam as some of the students forgot to strike their instruments when they spotted their mothers, others dropped devices, some pummeled their gadgets to a different beat, and others struggled to line up in order. But, their happy, glowing, smiling faces obliterated any flaws. They helped each other by retrieving instruments from the floor, adjusting a wayward costume, reminding each other where they should be in the line.

After a few musical numbers, the students put their instruments aside, and the mothers were invited to join them in song and dance to a recorded tune. Their exuberance was contagious as we joined them on the cafeteria floor. It was the ideal way to end the party.

As I drove home, I couldn't help thinking about the extraordinary amount of energy and effort that each student put into their performance. My heart ached when I thought about how little effort it took for us *normal* people to achieve, so easily, what they worked so hard to do. An idea was forming in my mind.

Sitting in the family room, curled up in my favorite easy chair, with my tablet and pencil, I thought about the young people that I had just watched work so hard to perform for their mothers. I scribbled notes on the paper, as I envisioned the awkward, shaking hands, the stumbling, shuffling feet, the wobbling, ungainly legs, the clumsy, unwieldy tongues.

Tears lingered in the corners of my eyes and gradually escaped down my cheeks.

Then I remembered their faces. I relived the lustrous sparkle that emanated from their eyes. I basked in the affection of their warm smiles. I reveled in the glow of their innocent, trusting, sincere faces. I admired their resolve and persistence.

I dried my tears. They didn't want or need my pity. They deserved my acceptance and appreciation.

I finished writing:

THE SPECIAL ONES

Their hands struggle to meet and make the sound;
I barely notice mine touch.
They wobble precariously as we rock;
I sway back and forth gracefully.
Their legs quiver in an attempt to stamp their feet;
Mine follow in a rhythmic pattern.
They sing a song in mumbled, jumbled words;
I sing out loud and clear.
We finish the song and they applaud themselves.
And rightfully they should,
For I have made no appreciable effort,
But they have given their all.

I promised myself that I would never forget how *special* the food and entertainment was that day. I would never forget how much energy and effort it took for those *special* ones just to get through an ordinary day. I would never forget how accepting and forgiving they were of each other. I thanked God for my *special* one.

❧

*Hope is some extraordinary spiritual
Grace that God gives us to control our fears,
Not to oust them.*

Vincent McNabb

❧

After the seizure that happened on the way home from the hospital, they began to escalate in frequency and intensity. One Saturday morning, in the middle of November, Stephanie collapsed on the kitchen floor and began contorting with brutal force. She thrashed, rolled, and battered her limbs violently. It seemed to go on forever. When her movement subsided, we placed her on the sofa. We crumbled beside her, emotionally exhausted. Jennifer stood watching, her face in fixed astonishment. This was the first time she had witnessed her sister's battle with a seizure.

Later, that same day, Jennifer, on her way to the college library, still upset about Stephanie, and mentally distracted, had an accident that totaled her car. When I heard the policeman's voice on the phone, my body shivered and my mind raced. Was she okay? Where was she?

He explained that she was frightened and nervous, but she wasn't seriously injured. "She was very fortunate," he stated.

I hung my head and wept tears of relief.

And then, the same week, before we could catch our breath from everything else that was happening, Robyn, who was five months pregnant, called to say that they had to have her baby aborted because the umbilical cord had wrapped around his neck, and he had died in her womb. It was the little boy they had wanted to add to their family of three girls.

I collapsed in the kitchen chair. My first instinct was to hurry to her side, but she assured me that she and Jim were dealing with it and they would be fine, and she was sorry to add to all of the problems we were already facing.

I put my head down on the table and wept tears of despair.

Then the question that Stephanie asked me, about two weeks after her Gramma's death, crept through my mind. *'Mommy, will we ever be happy again?'*

We were all devastated. The tension inside of us was building to an insurmountable crescendo. How much more could happen to our family? We jumped every time the phone rang. We flinched every time there was a knock on the door. We lay awake at night trying to close out the fear and pain that seemed to haunt us. We struggled to concentrate on our jobs. We questioned when, how, and if it would ever end. I wondered, were these happenings a mere premonition of worse things to come?

We started our trip to see Dr. Turner with heavy hearts. Unlike most of our visits to hospitals filled with questions and threats of revolt, Stephanie sat in the back seat, not even talking to George. We hadn't discussed the seriousness of this trip with her, but she seemed to sense our trepidation.

As we neared the hospital, gray, gloomy clouds filled the sky, meeting and meshing with the dark pavement of the road. Tiny droplets of cold rain collected on the windshield and then disappeared, swept away by the swish of the toiling wipers.

The heater hummed, laboring to warm the inside of the car. I longed for that warmth to penetrate me.

We walked down the long hallway to Dr. Turner's office passing patients' rooms, the familiar, stifling odor of antiseptics, medications, and disease filtering into the corridor, filling our nostrils. Stephanie clutched my hand and pressed her body tight against my leg.

I had an overwhelming urge to bolt and run. I wanted to conceal Stephanie under my heavy, water-proof parka. I wanted to encase all of my family inside of an impenetrable protective shield and escape to some distant, little-known island where bad things could never reach us. Instead, we took Stephanie to the playroom where she would be looked after while we were in our meeting.

Dr. Turner, clad in a cardigan sweater, came into his office carrying a large folder. He placed it on his desk, unopened, and sat with his chin resting on the knuckles of his folded hand, his eyes fixed on the report.

We sat waiting. I studied his face for some small hint or clue.

Opening the folder, he absent-mindedly ran his fingers over the top page, then lifted his head and frowned.

"I wish I had better news for you." His voice was subdued and sad. "But the tests show that Stephanie has a thalamic glioma with diffused gliomatosis cerebra." He closed the folder and walked around the desk, standing in front of us, his head bent, his eyes fastened on our faces.

My chest tightened. My eyes blurred. I couldn't see anything. I didn't want to hear anything.

I didn't understand the words, but I knew what he was describing was serious.

I shifted in my chair. I shivered. If I closed my eyes could I hide from Dr. Turner and what he was saying the way Stephanie hid from me?

"What that means in laymen's terms is that the tumor is located in the center of the brain. It's a large tumor with roots that are branching out into other parts of her brain."

He paused.

I was numb, yet every part of my body pulsated with each word that he spoke. I stared at him, but I couldn't see him. Blood pounded in my ears. His voice came from a great distance, an immense vacuum. Tears stung my eyes.

"Unfortunately, the tumor is so deep-seated that we cannot do a biopsy, so we have to assume that it is malignant. It also means that the tumor is inoperable."

Tumor. Malignant. Inoperable. Tumor. Malignant. Inoperable. TUMOR! MALIGNANT! INOPERABLE! My head was going to explode. I kept staring, but not seeing.

The room was spinning.

"I have never seen a tumor quite like this one." He returned to his chair and, with a pained expression on his face, he asked, "Do you have any questions for me?"

There was a long, uneasy pause.

"If the tumor is inoperable, can it be treated in any other way?" My question came out in a raspy whisper.

"Yes, we can give her radiation." He placed his elbows on the desk and gathered his hands beneath his chin. "However, my concern right now is that there's a tremendous amount of pressure on her brain because of the size of the tumor and a buildup of fluid. I'd like to confer with an oncology surgeon, have him look at all of her records, examine her, and then go from there."

Ronnie raised his head with a puzzled look on his face. "But you said the tumor is inoperable. Why does an oncology surgeon have to see her?"

There was another long, uneasy pause.

Dr. Turner sighed. "It's possible that we'll have to remove part of her brain to give room for the tumor."

REMOVE . . . BRAIN . . . GIVE ROOM . . . I clutched the seat of the chair and pressed my arms against my sides trying to stop my body from shaking. There's something wrong, I thought. I'm not hearing right. Remove her brain?

"If the tumor keeps putting pressure on the brain, it can push the brain down to touch the brain stem at the base of the spinal cord, and then . . ." Dr. Turner shrugged his shoulders and hesitated . . . "That would be the end. It would cause death."

It was too much to hear. It was too much to absorb. It was too much to process. It was a raging inferno inside of me.

There were more questions, more explanations, but it all became a blur. I couldn't get past those fateful words. *TUMOR. MALIGNANT. INOPERABLE.*

And, again, I remembered what Stephanie had said to me about a week after her Gramma's death. *Mommy, will we ever be happy again?*

The ride home was deafening in its silence.

What was there to say? Essentially, without articulating the word *terminal,* Dr. Turner had pronounced Stephanie's death sentence.

How do you break such devastating news to your other children? I couldn't call Robyn on the phone and break down and cry. And I would cry. I'd never get it said, and she'd rush home to be with us, in a frantic state of mind.

And Jennifer? She was a college student. She should be enjoying her classes and her friends. She should be worry free. She should be care free. She shouldn't have to deal with such devastating news.

I worried and fretted, trying to decide the most compassionate way to tell them.

Finally, I decided that I would arrange for them to come for dinner on Saturday, and we would tell them then. Stephanie and I would be leaving the following day to return to the hospital.

As I packed for both of us, I thought of Stephanie's first stay in this same hospital many years ago, at the age of twelve.

It had bothered her many physicians that they couldn't categorize Stephanie's mental retardation. They knew she wasn't Downs Syndrome, but they didn't know anything else about her condition. They suggested that we take her to a major hospital in Baltimore for a thorough examination and analysis.

I propped myself up against the headboard of the bed and opened the journal that I had kept from her first stay.

Day 1—Sunday

Wow! What a start to Stephanie's stay at the hospital. She is so scared. She cried and screamed every time somebody came into her room. I finally asked Ronnie to stay with her for a few minutes while I ran down to the gift shop. I needed to get her something to make her happy and calm her down. I snatched a monkey from the shelf. I think it's called Curious George.

Stephanie is frightened even though no one has approached her with a needle (yet). Every time someone walks into the room her eyes get big and she looks at me. She's been promised that there won't be any shots today, but what about tomorrow and the day after, and the day after, and the day after . . .

She cries periodically, says she wants to go home. She has colored some and played some with Tommy and Raggedy Ann, but George seems to have stolen her heart.

Even George isn't occupying her mind enough to keep her from thinking about being in the hospital. I have just about run out of things to say to reassure her. She asks questions that, if I answer her truthfully, will make her even more frightened and upset. But, I can't lie to her for then she'll not trust me or anyone else again. So, I hedge, I talk around the questions, and I tell bits and pieces of truth.

I stuck my finger in between the pages to save the spot where I was reading, rested my head on the pillows and closed my eyes. I was going to have to do the same thing this time that I had done so many years ago. I would hedge, I would talk around her questions, I would tell her bits and pieces of truth, but this was going to be so much more difficult. This was so much more serious.

From down the hallway in Stephanie's bedroom, I could hear her singing along with Kenny Rogers. Listening to her singing, oblivious to what might be happening soon, tore at my heart, and I knew right then that I wouldn't tell her even a part of the truth.

And I knew I wouldn't tell the whole truth to Robyn and Jennifer. I would tell them as much as they needed to know, which was that we were going to meet with several doctors to decide what should be done about the tumor that was growing inside of Stephanie's head. Not a complete lie.

I opened the journal and read on.

A helper from the playroom heard her crying and came in and invited her to play. The tears stopped immediately.

I checked on her every commercial during the ball game, but she told me she didn't need me. That's nice for a while, though I continued to check on her. It seemed strange, even disappointing, to hear her tell me that she didn't need me. I'm beginning to think that I'm as dependent on her as she is on me.

Did I, surreptitiously, derive pleasure from knowing that she would always be dependent on me?

I put the journal down on the bed next to me and stared at my reflection in the dresser mirror. I looked intently into my own eyes, searching for the truth.

I painstakingly walked through every disheartening revelation during her infancy, every disillusioning attempt to help her perform at her age level, the unsatisfactory information-gathering hospital stay, every revealing doctor's office visit, the intense, all-consuming program from the Institutes, the solemn declarations after each psychologist's testing session, the disappointing results of regular classroom placement.

Then my mind journeyed back to the present, and I felt the weight of a disquieting realization. While my heart ached for Stephanie and all that she would be denied in her lifetime, I found that, after the initial shock, pain and despondency of learning of her *problems*, I quickly resolved myself to the inevitability of her condition and what it would mean for the rest of *my* life.

And I *wasn't un*happy.

Was I, am I, as dependent on Stephanie as she was, is, on me? I didn't know if it could be considered a dependency, but it certainly was a need. I needed to have her to look after. I needed to have her to nurture. I needed her to need me. *Was I secretly glad that she was a perpetual child?*

I averted my eyes.

I could no longer look at myself.

Day 2—Monday

I'm not sure why I'm keeping this journal. I guess I'm afraid that I'll forget everything, once we get back home.

I took the journal with me and walked down to the kitchen and made myself a cup of mint tea. I sat at the table, warming my hands, my fingers cradling the cup.

I wondered why I had kept a journal of her first stay. Ordinarily, I'm not a journal person. I had always admired people who took the time to record their thoughts, their feelings, their experiences in journals, but I never felt the need to do it, before this.

Then I realized that, in a sense, I'd been keeping a journal all of Stephanie's life. I had every paper, every record, every documentation, every confirmation, every verification of every situation, every circumstance that we experienced with Stephanie from the beginning.

Each time—period in our lives was marked by remembering *when Stephanie* did this, said that, participated in this, competed in that, learned how to do this, learned how to do that, had to see this doctor, had to see that doctor, started this program, went to this school.

Would I keep a journal this time? Yes. I tucked it under my arm and carried my cup upstairs to the bedroom.

Had to leave the playroom abruptly. An aide came and said there was a doctor in Steph's room waiting to see her. He is a geneticist. He was very polite, but as usual he asked the same questions that every other doctor has asked from Thursday on. Was I sick during my pregnancy? Did I take any medications during my pregnancy? Are my husband and I related, outside of our marriage of course. I know them by heart. I could answer them before they ask. I want to tell them I have answered these questions many, many times before, so why don't they check Steph's records and save us both some time. Of course, I don't.

And each time that they ask me these questions, I feel guilty. I don't know why, because I didn't do anything wrong. Intellectually I can understand why they ask these questions. Emotionally, I reject them. They are scientists. Everything has a reason.

There is a 'why' to everything, coupled with their need to know, their chance to garner knowledge for future use, future generations.

I am a mother. The why, the need and the opportunity are all unnecessary to me unless there is some hope attached to them. Not hope for the future, but hope for now, for me, for mine.

The geneticist's examination was similar to how the other doctors examined Steph, but he seemed especially curious about her limbs. He checked her feet and her toes. He examined her fingers and spent considerable time staring at her palms. I wanted to ask him if he saw anything interesting in her future and could he read my palms and tell me my future, but I was afraid he wouldn't appreciate my humor. And, perhaps, he sees more in Steph's palm than I care to know right now. And my future? Steph's future is my future.

Tuesday—more tests, more doctors, more lab work, etc. Steph is not one bit pleased with all that's happening. She's so scared. Because it's a teaching hospital, doctors come in clusters. When they surround her bed, Steph looks like an ensnared animal. Her eyes dart from one side of the bed to the other. Then she fastens her eyes on me and silently pleads for protection. I hold her hand and stroke her arm. I feel so helpless. I find that I'm ambivalent. I want to protect her, but I also want the doctors to have the opportunity to examine her and determine what they can do for her, if anything.

I wonder. Where do you draw the line? When do you say enough is enough? When do you decide that you must make the decision NOT to put Steph through any more fear and pain?

I closed my eyes and leaned my head back onto the pillows. We were getting ready to take Steph to the hospital for something so much more serious than what she had experienced with her first visit.

Would we have to make a decision to draw the line? Would we have to say *enough is enough?* Could we put our own selfish needs and wants aside and do what was right and good for Stephanie?

I knew Ronnie could, but I wasn't sure about myself.

Thursday—Going home

Our meeting with the doctors was depressing. The bottom line? They still can't categorize Steph's retardation. They called it "a freak of nature." They did tell us that our other children had very little chance of carrying a defective gene and having mentally retarded children. Not much help for Steph. Maybe I should have asked the doctor to read my palm.

I'm not sure what it feels like to be depressed, but I think I am.

I guess I'm glad that I didn't ask the doctor to read Stephanie's palm, or mine either, I thought. What if I had known what was in the future for us? Would I have done anything differently?

At dinner, on Saturday evening, Ronnie and I launched into nervous chatter, asking five—year—old Liz and four—year—old Sarah about their home-schooling lessons, one-and-a-half year old Abby about her baby dolls, Jennifer about her classes, Jim about his latest political views, Robyn about the advantages of teaching her children at home, and anything else we could think of to divert everyone's attention from the elephant in the room.

I felt like a one-handed juggler just trying to keep the conversation aloft. I had no appetite, so I pushed my food around on the plate, hoping that no one noticed.

Our forced gaiety soon wore thin and rang hollow.

I could see by the looks on the girls' faces that they sensed that we had something important to tell them. They knew we had been to the hospital to talk to the doctors.

They knew that it couldn't be good news or I would have blurted it out gleefully. They also knew that our dinners together were customarily on Sundays.

After dessert, Stephanie had disappeared upstairs to play with George and listen to her Kenny Rogers tapes, and the little ones gravitated to the TV set and the toys in the family room.

We sat at the table, the leftovers of our meal still scattered about. I checked to see if anyone wanted seconds on dessert, making a last-ditch effort to delay what I didn't want to do.

Finally, I cleared my throat and plunged into the conversation. I told them what Dr. Turner had told us, even the need to remove part of Stephanie's brain. It all came spewing out of my mouth like hot lava. I used the terms *malignant* and *inoperable*. The words continued to tumble out of my mouth.

Their chins quivered, tears ran down their faces, they fidgeted, folding and unfolding their napkins in their laps, their eyes looked everywhere but at me as I continued my diatribe. Relief settled over me. I couldn't stop myself until they knew everything.

I moved from one to the other, hugging them, reminding them that we had to be strong and keep our thoughts positive. I asked them to pray for a miracle. But nothing I said could stop the flow of their tears or mine.

Ronnie and Jim, their faces flushed with emotion, moved awkwardly around the table touching shoulders, stroking arms, mumbling words of consolation.

Now, Jennifer, with her head down, sat with her hands clasped under her chin, and I thought of the day that she, then eleven years old, started looking at Stephanie as her friend and sister rather than a competitor. Though Jennifer hadn't been blatant about her jealousy, there were subtle indications that she wasn't thrilled with the attention given to Stephanie. It wasn't easy being the youngest child and, yet, having to vie with your older sister for the position of *baby* of the family.

She would say . . . *'Why doesn't Stephanie have to pull weeds in the flower garden? Why does Stephanie get to wear her good shoes to school? Why do you yell at me when my room's messy, but don't yell at Stephanie?'* These questions infiltrated most of Jennifer's conversations during her childhood years, and I spent many hours trying to explain Stephanie's lack of understanding and coordination, and her need for special attention.

Then, one day I knew Jennifer had turned the corner. We walked into the Acme, grabbed a cart, and started down the aisle. Jennifer squeezed my arm. "Mom, look. They're staring at Stephanie."

I turned my gaze in the direction of Jennifer's glare. There were three teenage girls looking and pointing at Stephanie. "It's okay. Don't let it bother you." I tried to move on.

"But, Mom, they're makin' fun of Stephanie. If they don't stop, I'm goin over there and punch em out." She continued to glare at the girls, balled her hand into a fist, and put her arm around Stephanie's shoulders.

"It's okay, honey, they just don't understand. They don't have a *special* sister like you do." My eyes watered with pride.

And now it was Sunday. Stephanie clung to George as we drove to the hospital.

Waiting. Paper work. Questions. Waiting. People bustling in and out of the room.

Introductions. Questions. Blood pressure. Temperature. Examination. Move a cot into the room. Finally we were settled in. Stephanie was still clinging to George.

They wouldn't wait until Monday to do another MRI. There was concern in the knitted eyebrows, scowling pursed lips. "I think we need to get an MRI today. If there's an increase in the swelling, as I suspect, we'll want to get Stephanie started on steroids." Dr. Turner sat on the edge of the bed, pointing his flashlight into Stephanie's eyes.

Not so fast, I wanted to plead. Slow down. Stephanie looked good. Her skin was pink, her eyes still sparkled, her smile still glowed. Why couldn't she be as good on the inside as she looked on the outside?

They hustled her out of the room with Ronnie and me trailing behind. "Mommy, Mommy, what're they gonna do? I'm scared Mommy." Stephanie reached from the rolling cot, searching for my hand.

I grasped her tiny fingers and intertwined them with mine. I was scared too. The urgency with which they were responding to her examination was alarming. "It's okay, honey, they just want to do another test. You've done this test before. You won't feel a thing." I kissed her soft, warm cheek as they whisked her away.

You won't feel a thing.

How many *things* would Stephanie never have the opportunity to feel, experience, achieve?

Ever.

See, I am sending an angel ahead
Of you to guard you along the way.

Exodus 23:20

We had just enough time to dash to the store and pick up the bags of bubble gum, which the girls on the softball team chewed incessantly, before we had to get to softball practice. "Isn't it a great day? The sky's blue, the grass is green, the breeze is warm." I drove out the lane, turned left and headed into town.

"Mommy," Stephanie said, patiently, "the sky is *always* blue and the grass is *always* green." She sat in the back seat, holding George, as usual.

"Not all of the time, is it Jennifer?" I glanced to my right where Jennifer sat clutching her glove.

"Not always," she replied.

"And the air isn't always warm this early in the spring like it is today. Open your window and let the air blow on your face. You'll see." I peeked over my shoulder to see if she was rolling down the window.

"Ooh, it feels good Mommy. I like it when it's warm. Mommy, ya know what?" Stephanie leaned up and put her elbows on the back of my seat in her excitement.

"What?"

"I'm really happy."

I looked in the rear view mirror and saw the sparkle in her eyes and the smile dancing all over her face. "Oh, I'm so glad that you're happy. It makes me happy when you're happy."

"Ya, know what else?" The enthusiasm was building in her voice.

"No. You tell me."

"I'm gonna get married some day. I'm gonna marry Todd."

My heart skipped a beat. Todd, a sweet Downs Syndrome boy, was a classmate of Stephanie's and the son of friends of ours.

I could feel Jennifer's uneasy gaze on my face. I swallowed, cleared my throat, and hesitated. "Well, Steph, I'm not sure about you getting married." My mind raced, seeking the right words. "I just don't know how I'd get along without you. I need you to stay and live with Daddy and me. We'd really miss you if you went away."

"Well, I can get married and not go away. We can live with you." She smiled. Problem solved.

"Maybe we can talk about it later, but you're only fifteen, much too young to get married."

"Okay, but we hafta make up our minds soon, cause someday I wanna have a baby. Then George'll have somebody to play with."

I felt a heaviness settle like a winter cloak and spread throughout my body. Oh, my baby, I thought, there will be so many things that you won't be able to do, and you'll never understand why.

Several weeks later, when an older sister of one of my ball players gave birth to a baby girl, Stephanie broached the subject again. "Mommy, how old do ya hafta be to get married and have a baby?"

Once again, I braced myself, hoping to find the right words. "Stephie, honey, you're different from lots of the other kids, and you just won't be able to have babies."

Stephanie gave me a bewildered look. "*Why* am *I* different?"

Think of something to say. "You're different because you're our Special Angel."

"What's a Special Angel?"

"A Special Angel is someone that God chooses to come to earth and make people happy. And you make us *very* happy. So we don't want you to leave us."

"But, I already told you that I can live here with you and Dad. Me 'n' Todd . . . *and* the baby." Her voice held a hint of exasperation.

"I know my Special Angel, but don't you think that George and Paul and all of your other dolls are enough? They keep you really busy."

How would I ever explain to her that being different meant not living life like everybody else?

They rolled Stephanie back into her room. She was still groggy from the medication that kept her motionless during the MRI.

"Dr. Turner will be in to talk to you in a little while." The nurse straightened Steph's pillow beneath her head. I nodded.

Stephanie slept. Ronnie nervously surfed the TV channels. This was real. This wasn't happening to someone else. It was happening to us, and ignoring it wasn't going to make it go away. I was good at ignoring unpleasant issues, but not this one. I felt like I was suffocating. Things were happening too fast. Would they really remove a part of her brain?

Dr. Turner came into the room, his fatigued shoulders slumping and his cocoa-brown hair falling across his forehead. He sat down on the edge of Stephanie's bed and placed his hand on her arm. He seemed to be gathering his thoughts. "As I suspected," he began, "there is intracranial pressure, or brain swelling. The brain rests inside a bone case, so when it swells, it experiences even more trauma than the tumor is causing. The more damage the brain receives the more oxygen it needs and the more it swells. The brain is housed inside of the skull, and there's no room to expand. We can, temporarily, give some relief by administering steroids." He stopped, adjusted his position on the bed, and sighed. "This is, as I said, a temporary solution." He looked at Ronnie. He looked at me. Did we understand what he was intimating?

The next afternoon I sat in Dr. Turner's office, where we were scheduled to meet the surgeon who would perform the right temporal lobectomy that was no longer a choice, my hands pressed together on my lap and my jaws clamped shut tight to keep my chin from quivering.

Ronnie sat staring into space.

Trying to distract myself, I counted the black and white tiles on the floor. Were there more white than black tiles? Were there more black than white tiles? Were there an even number? Did all of the rooms and hallways in the hospital have the same color tiles? I'd never noticed. I'd have to remember to look. I counted the acoustic ceiling tiles. There were fewer tiles overhead because they were larger, and they were all white.

I looked around the room. Who picked out the pictures hanging on the wall, I wondered? They were copies of Norman Rockwell paintings. Probably his wife, I thought. Did Dr. Turner have a wife? I never noticed if he wore a wedding band. Frantically, I looked for something else to attach my mind to. What am I doing? Counting tiles? Determining who might have chosen pictures on a doctor's office walls?

How do I keep my world from crashing down around me? How do I go on in a world that is oblivious to the fact that my life is spinning out of control? I looked at my watch. Dr. Turner and Dr. Oliver were late. We might have so little time left. How dare they waste it.

Stephanie was in the playroom with an aide. She wanted to come to Dr. Turner's office with us, but he had been very specific. He didn't want Stephanie present while we were discussing the surgery and what would follow. I knew he was right, but I wanted to spend every minute I could with her.

From my angle, in his office, I could see the everyday hustle-bustle of the hospital. Doctors, nurses, technicians, aides, and visitors, all scurrying up and down the hallways, all on a mission, all consumed with their own duties and responsibilities, all oblivious to the fear and trepidation emanating from Ronnie and me. I watched to see if anyone glanced through the open doorway. I wondered if anybody even knew we were here. I wondered if anybody even cared.

"I'm sorry we're late." Dr. Turner rushed into the room with a handful of papers and manila envelopes. "This is Dr. Oliver." He pointed to the gangly, disheveled dark-haired man who followed him into the room.

He nodded in our direction and, with deft and precision, fastened the x-rays onto the lighted screen. "I'm sure that Dr. Turner has shown you these pictures before, but I want to outline and discuss the growth of the tumor and what it means as far as a diagnosis and prognosis is concerned."

Diagnosis. Prognosis.

The room was closing in around me. Dr. Oliver was going to describe, in detail, what I'd been trying to deny for weeks. I must hear. I must absorb. I must accept.

"The tumor growing inside of Stephanie's skull takes up space, which increases the pressure inside of her head." He pointed to the first film. "It's this pressure that is causing her headaches and seizures. Unfortunately, we cannot operate on the tumor because of its location. Therefore, the next step for us is to reduce the swelling with the use of steroids."

He embarked on a detailed description of the names, purposes, and side-effects of the medications that they would use on Stephanie, explaining that the side-effects were temporary and would disappear when the medication ceased.

"As much as we would like to proceed quickly with Stephanie's surgery, we feel that it's necessary to have her on steroids for a period of time before we operate because, immediately after the surgery, swelling can increase inside of the skull." He pointed to the second film, outlining the edges of her tumor. "So, steroids first, and then . . ." He hesitated.

I was struggling to concentrate on what he was saying, then, suddenly, his words penetrated and echoed inside my head. "We know that, without the surgery to remove the right frontal lobe of Stephanie's brain, there is *little hope* that Stephanie will survive for any length of time."

He paused again, waiting for us to grasp the enormity of what he had just said.

LITTLE HOPE. LITTLE HOPE. LITTLE HOPE. The words ricocheted inside me. Again, I was suffocating. I heard his words floating around the room from a distance.

"After surgery . . . radiation therapy . . . radiation oncologist . . . external beam . . . directly aimed at the tumor . . . fractionated into many small doses . . . given over a period of time . . . five to seven weeks . . . side-effects . . . fatigue, loss of appetite, nausea, short-term memory loss, brain edema, skin rash, hair loss . . . radiation therapy can also cause swelling . . ."

No more. No more. Please stop. A small voice inside of me was pleading with him.

I blinked my eyes, trying to focus. Dr. Oliver was asking us if we had any questions. "With the removal of the right frontal brain and the radiation therapy, what is Stephanie's prognosis?" As I waited for his answer, my heart raced.

"We can't predict the effectiveness of the radiation therapy. But, we do know that, regardless of how much time we can buy with the treatments, the end result of Stephanie's tumor will be *terminal*."

TERMINAL! There, he said it. No more skirting the issue. No more false hope.

All of those tiles that I had counted were crushing the life out of me. I had to get out of that room. I had to get to Stephanie.

I rushed down the hall to the playroom, pain and fear crushing my chest. I leaned against the wall, shivering, fighting back the sobs that were gathering in my throat.

When I moved into the doorway, Stephanie saw me and hurried to my side. "I was wonderin' when you'd come back, Mommy. I'm tired of playin'. Can we go home?" She wrapped her skinny arms around my waist and pressed her head against me.

I blinked my eyes and forced a smile. "Not yet, honey. We're going to have to stay for a little while longer. But we *will* take you home. I promise."

Strange that Dr. Oliver would apply the words *buying time* to someone's life expectancy. If only it were that simple. If only we could go to the store, buy some time, freeze it, or can it, or hoard it in our pantry, and retrieve it when we needed it. If only we could go back throughout our lifetime and reclaim all of the time we had wasted and place it in a savings account to be used in a desperate situation. If only we could allocate our excess time to someone we loved, someone who was *running out* of time. If only . . . If only . . . If only . . .

Five days later, we *were* going home. Stephanie was responding well to the steroids, and we could administer them to her orally. In the car, she maintained a constant chatter with George and her father. She was headed home and she was happy.

We hadn't told her about the upcoming surgery. How do you tell your twenty-five year old daughter, who operates on the level of a five or six—year—old child, that she is going to have a part of her brain taken out?

At home, we watched for any changes in her behavior that might indicate that the steroids weren't working to relieve the pressure on her brain. And, aside from sleepiness and dizziness from the seizure medications, and an increased appetite from the steroids, everything seemed to stay the same.

It appeared that we *were* buying some time.

Music is well said to be the speech of angels.

Thomas Carlyle

The phone rang. How I hated to hear the phone ring. Was it more bad news? I was relieved to hear that it was my niece, Pam, and not one of Stephanie's doctors.

She was calling to tell me that Kenny Rogers was going to be appearing at a music theater in the area. She was hoping that we would make an attempt to get tickets and take Stephanie to see her idol.

"Oh, I don't know Pam. We never know how Stephanie's going to be each day. Most days she's asleep by seven o'clock. And, I doubt that we'd even be able to get tickets."

"But, Aunt Carole, you have to try. And who knows when Kenny Rogers will be in this area again?"

The enthusiasm in her voice had turned to a desperate plea. We both knew that she wasn't thinking about whether Kenny Rogers would be around, but whether Stephanie would be around.

Three days later it was all set. We were not only going to the concert, but we were going to have dinner first at a nearby restaurant. My trepidation slowly turned into anticipation. Ronnie and Jennifer were getting as eager about our trip as I was, but we couldn't tell Stephanie yet. She would get too excited, and we worried that it could trigger a seizure.

Finally, I couldn't hold off any longer. I told her a week before the concert. She hopped, skipped, jumped up and down, danced, giggled, laughed, clapped her hands, and shouted. "When are we goin' Mommy? How far is it? Where are we gonna eat?" Her enthusiasm was contagious. We found ourselves grinning from ear to ear.

I wanted to make this a happy, exciting time for her. I wanted this to be a positive memory for all of us. I promised myself that I would make this an occasion that we would cherish and store in our memory bank.

Dr. Oliver was buying time.

I would store memories.

Memories. Memories. There were so many good memories from our camping trips that Stephanie loved but tired of after three or four days, wanting to return to the comfort of her home. How could I ever forget Stephanie sitting with us in a large circle around the campfire on our camping trips? I saw her making her rounds from beach chair to beach chair talking to everybody, carrying her Dr Pepper, sometimes stopping to sit with an aunt or an uncle, a cousin or a friend, but always she would make her way back to me. Cuddling up on my lap, she would wind down from the day's activities, and I would know that it wouldn't be long before she'd ask her father to take her to bed.

I thought too of the camping trip when a group of us went golfing, and when we approached a hole that had the tee on one side of a small pond and the green on the other side, and my sister, Helen, a first-time golfer, ended up putting three balls in the pond.

Stephanie, who had been watching us intently, said, "Boy, Mommy, Aunt Helen is really good. She got three balls in the water and you didn't get any in."

We roared with laughter. She made her Aunt Helen's day.

And I pictured yet another camping trip, when we traveled over three hours, with Jennifer, her friend Tabitha and her cousin Michael chattering in the back of the van, and Stephanie talking to George, preparing him for what she thought would happen over the weekend. The excitement and elation inside the old black van was palpable.

When we reached the small town that was closest to the campground, I began searching for the sign that I expected to see that would lead us to the entrance. No sign. Perhaps we had made a wrong turn. At this point, Ronnie was getting tired of driving and more than a little frustrated as we rode around aimlessly.

Noticing that our verbal exchanges were tinged with anger and irritation as we discussed what we should do next, the chatter in the back seat had ceased. They were sensing the tension between us.

Ronnie steered the van into an American Legion building parking lot. He took the post card that had the confirmation number on it, and trudged towards the door.

As we sat waiting, I wondered if I had even checked the address on the card. But, why would I? We'd been to this campground a few years before.

When he returned to the van, I could see the storm clouds covering his face. The news wasn't good.

He climbed into the van and slammed the door. "The campground that was here fell into a huge sink hole. They bulldozed it under. The campground that we're *supposed* to go to is fifty miles from here. The address is *clearly* on the post card." His words were ice-laden.

He whipped the van out of the parking lot, the pop-up camper spraying shale and small pebbles as he sped down the highway and headed back in the direction from which we came. An uneasy silence permeated the air.

And then, Stephanie, who had been quietly watching and listening to what was taking place, held George up in front of her face, and declared, "Well, George, there goes our vacation." We all burst out laughing. The tension was broken. We had fifty miles to go.

I contacted Dr. Turner, told him about our plans for the concert, and asked him if I would do any harm to Stephanie if I withheld her seizure medication until after it was over; I didn't want her to fall asleep before the concert even started.

He didn't answer the question with the conviction that I'd hoped he would. "It's never good to mess with the schedule of medication, but I understand why you're considering it." He paused. "After all, how often do you get to see Kenny Rogers in concert?"

. . . *how often do you get to see Kenny Rogers in concert?* I knew what he meant just like I knew what Pam meant when she urged me to get tickets. Going to the concert was going to be bitter-sweet.

117

Finally, the big day arrived. Jennifer and Stephanie were in the back seat of the car chatting about the concert and calculating how much time was left of our hour-and-a-half—long trip when Jennifer, her voice rising with anxiety said, "Mom, she's starting. She's having a seizure."

Ronnie was already scrambling over the seat as I veered off to the side of the road. He held her shaking body against his chest until she relaxed. I sat, hunched over the steering wheel, asking myself why I had done such a fool-hardy, risky thing as withholding the medication. Would she have more seizures? Should we continue on to the concert?

We sat along the side of the road trying to decide what we should do, when Stephanie spoke up. "I'm not goin' home without seein' Kenny." Miss Independence made the decision for us.

We sat in the restaurant perusing the menu. "I know what I'm havin," Stephanie announced. "I'm havin meatloaf, mashed potatoes, apple sauce, and chocolate milk. And for dessert I'm havin' chocolate cake." Smugly, she placed the menu on the table.

We glanced at each other. Her speech was clearer than usual, and she appeared more alert than she had been in weeks.

As Ronnie pushed Stephanie down the aisle in her wheelchair towards our seats, and she saw the decorations, her eyes glowed and darted around the room. Small Christmas trees, adorned with bright—colored lights and glittering gold and silver balls, surrounded the performance area, white lights illuminated and circled the stage, green wreaths with red bows and pine cones covered the walls, and Christmas carols were being piped over the sound system.

Stephanie grinned and squirmed in her seat as the Christmas carols faded and Kenny's band took the stage. The lights dimmed, and then, suddenly, Kenny appeared singing and waving amid the roar of approval from the audience.

Stephanie clapped her hands and squealed, "Mommy, Mommy, there's Kenny. There he is." She pointed, following him with her tiny, crooked index finger as he moved around the stage.

She bounced in her seat, grabbed my hand, kissed it, and sang along when the band struck up *Lucille*, her favorite. Happy tears filled my eyes.

Her eyes glistened, and a radiant smile spread across her face as Kenny transitioned from one hit to the next.

She knew the words and sang along with: *Ruby, Don't Take Your Love to Town; Through the Years; She Believes in Me; For the Good Times; You Decorated My Life.*

She kept glancing at me. Was I listening? Was I enjoying?

As the intensity of the concert increased, Stephanie began to cry, so I lifted her onto my lap. I could feel her body shudder and quake with the stimulation of the music and lights. I was afraid she might have a seizure.

But then the concert shifted into Christmas songs and the tempo and intensity of the music lessened, and I could feel her body relax against me. She spent the rest of the concert snuggled in my arms, her head resting on my shoulder.

When the concert was over and we made our way through the parking lot, the sky, filled with glowing stars and a radiant moon, seemed to reflect the inside of the theater and the joy that Stephanie felt. She cradled her program on her lap, the featured picture of Kenny staring up at her. She was physically exhausted, slumping to one side in her wheelchair, but her face sparkled like the stars above us.

We sat in a long line of traffic, inching our way out of the parking lot. Stephanie kept up a running account of what she had experienced.

"Mommy, didya hear when Kenny sang *Lucille*? I sang with him. Didya hear me? I liked when Kenny sang *Ruby,* cause he did funny things with his voice." Excitement poured from her mouth and floated in the night air.

As I drove, I thought about Christmas, now only weeks away. Would it be our last one together, I wondered, as memories flooded through me.

I thought of the Christmas when Stephanie was eagerly waiting a call from Santa. She had her list ready. Yes, it had been changed several times, as usual, but it had remained the same long enough for me to feel confident that she was sure of what she wanted. I had completed my shopping.

When the phone rang, Stephanie snatched it up, waving her scrap of paper in front of her.

"HO, HO, HO, this is Santa Claus. Have you been a good girl Stephanie? Have you been helping your Mommy?" Our friend, Bub, was making his yearly call.

"Yes, Santa. I empty the dishwasher, I fold clothes, I make my own bed, and I take care of George." She rattled off her inventory of chores triumphantly.

"Good girl. Now what do you want for Christmas?"

"Okay." She read from her list. "For George I wanna pair of shoes, a shirt and some pants, a hat, and a blanket for his bassinet. And I wanna puzzle, a new tape player and some tapes, some books, a coat and a hat, and a pair of shoes . . . . .and I wanna Cabbage Patch doll." She danced and giggled as she finished her list. "That's it, Santa. Thanks for callin me." She dropped the phone, pranced into the living room, and began telling her father all about her phone call.

I stood in the kitchen in shock. Until this very minute, she hadn't mentioned a Cabbage Patch doll. I'd been hearing that it was a hot Christmas item and was extremely difficult to find. And, at this late date? Probably impossible.

Robyn and I scoured the area, gradually expanding into the two neighboring states. We had one day left.

The phone rang. "Mom," I could hear the excitement in Robyn's voice, "I found the doll."

Another tightrope walk. Another save.

The stars had disappeared from the sky, and the moon was clouded over. It was spitting rain. I turned on the windshield wipers and glanced in the rearview mirror.

We were nearing home now, and everyone was still sleeping. I was enjoying the quiet and solitude. I was relishing the *time* to remember and *store* memories.

I pictured Stephanie, her skinny legs wobbling as she ran the fifty yard dash in Special Olympics, looking like she was running the race by herself because everyone else was so far ahead of her. I thought of the time in the long jump that she out—jumped a girl who was so tall she made Stephanie look like a midget. I saw her standing on the podium, smiling, her shoulders back, her arms flat against her sides, her head tilted forward, accepting a gold medal around her neck for throwing a softball farther than her competitors.

I visualized Stephanie, dressed in her Brownie Girl Scout uniform, standing at attention and oozing pride and self-esteem, while accepting her latest proficiency badge for completing another of her handicraft or service requirements.

And I pictured the look of joy and disbelief on Stephanie's face when Ronnie asked her if she would sing with him in church. I remembered how excited she was to spend time practicing with her father. I remembered how she fought to hold her head still when she stood in front of the congregation, smiling and smoothing her dress as she prepared to sing. I remembered the delight I felt looking at her beaming face and listening to them sing that Sunday morning.

My heart warmed as I thought about her many achievements.

She had accomplished far more than ride a bus by herself.

Dost thou love life?
Then do not squander time,
For that's the stuff life is made of.

Ben Franklin

Christmas came. We celebrated. I hadn't had much enthusiasm, shopping and decorating, but I wanted to keep things *as usual* for the rest of the family.

Stephanie made her list, which, of course, included clothes for George, but there weren't any last minute surprises. Clothes, puzzles, Kenny's latest tape. In recent years, her list never varied.

I kept a smile on my face, but my chest tightened around my aching heart, watching Stephanie, sitting propped up on the sofa with pillows, opening the gifts we carried to her. She was at the point now that, if she wasn't sitting in her wheelchair, we didn't trust that she could maintain her balance. No longer could she rummage beneath the tree with the girls, tearing paper from boxes, exclaiming excitedly over her latest surprise, holding it up in the air for all of us to see, because she thought we didn't know what Santa Claus had brought her.

We didn't voice our thoughts, but it was obvious when our eyes met that we all secretly wondered if this would be our last Christmas with Stephanie.

All through January, we ran back and forth to the hospital, having Stephanie checked. Was she any worse? It was never a question of whether she was any better.

"Mommy," Stephanie sidled up to me on the sofa and squirmed onto my lap, "will you sleep with me tonight?"

Would I sleep with *Miss Independence*? Would I sleep with the little girl who never wanted anybody in her bed? Would I sleep with the little girl who guarded her privacy by closing the door to her bedroom while she sat on the floor and listened to her favorite tapes, often singing along? Would I sleep with the little girl who wouldn't allow Jennifer to touch anything in her room? Would I enter her hallowed ground?

"Of course, I'll sleep with you, honey, but *why?*" This strange request made me nervous.

"I don't know. I just feel kinda funny. You don't mind sleepin' with me, do ya?" She snuggled closer and stroked my cheek.

"I don't mind at all, my Special Angel." As I pressed her head in the crook of my neck, a strange, strength-sapping weakness swept through me. Was her body telling her something we couldn't see?

Every day, for the next two weeks, Stephanie repeated her request, and I lay with her, my body curled around her in a fetal position. She smelled of strawberry shampoo, Johnson's baby lotion, and an occasional trace of lavender body spray that she liked to dab behind her ears. The soft and pliant skin on her delicate frame stretched over her bony ribs that I cupped with my hand. Her crooked index finger on her tiny right hand, which had a small, double-jointed curvature on the knuckle, rested on the pillow beside her face.

I lay in bed glancing around the room which wasn't completely dark. I saw the small chest sitting beneath the window where she kept her overstuffed pocketbook, her and George's toys, her books and tapes. I saw the top of her dresser covered with small bottles of cologne, costume jewelry, food coupons, and folded sheets of paper that were mostly notes to and from Carroll Mitchell. I saw George in his bassinet in the corner next to Stephanie's side of the bed. I saw the framed caricatures of Stephanie, one with her cat, and one with her softball glove, hanging on the wall over the head of the bed. I saw her closet door that never quite shut tight because she had so many shoes crammed in the bottom.

Would my memories of her fade with time?

I wanted to remember that despite the many pairs of shoes that she had in her closet, she chose to wear her black, high top, leather sneakers, with pink trim, with her shorts, her jeans, *and* her dresses when she could sneak behind my back. I wanted to remember that she drank her tea with milk and sugar and that she considered tea a cure-all for everything, physical and emotional. I wanted to remember that she could catch flies in her hand with one quick swipe, but would accidentally allow them to escape when she opened her hand to show me. I wanted to remember that she would kick and shout, Karate-style, when she was being teased by Jennifer. I wanted to remember that she ate the crispy, fried skin off chicken and left most of the white meat on her plate. I wanted to remember that she always asked for crabs and beer for her birthday dinner because she thought that was the thing to do in July. I wanted to remember that she ate spinach with butter and vinegar. I wanted to remember that she cocked her head to one side when she was trying to talk me into allowing her to do something. I wanted to remember that we wore our Penn State sweatshirts to watch Penn *Estate*, as she called the school, play football. I wanted to remember that she was afraid of vacuum cleaners and thunder and lightning. I wanted to remember that she liked to wrap her arms around my waist, stand on the top of my feet, and get a free ride while I worked around the kitchen. I wanted to remember that she loved getting butterfly kisses but found it difficult to give them. I wanted to remember that she often transposed syllables in words and would tell me that she had brought her *port recard* home and reminded Jennifer to *havebe* when she left the house. I wanted to remember that often on weekends I awakened to see her standing by the bed watching me sleep. I wanted to remember that, from the day I told her she was our *Special Angel*, she asked me over and over, everyday, *Am I your Special Angel?*

I wanted to breathe everything about her into my body. I wanted to drink in everything about her, fill my heart and mind.

Each morning I awoke relieved that nothing had happened during the night to justify the anxiety that caused my heart to pound and made me short of breath.

Then, one night I awoke with a warm sensation spreading over my legs. For a few seconds, I couldn't remember where I was. Then, I leaped out of bed, snapped on the light and quickly returned to the bed to examine Stephanie. As I threw back the covers, I could see that she had wet the bed.

"Oh no," I mumbled, as the realization hit me.

The tumor must be interfering with the function of the thalamus. Her condition was deteriorating. *When the tumor affects the thalamus, in the forebrain, it interferes with the processes and relays of sensory information that selectively go to various parts of the cerebral cortex.*

I remembered what Dr. Turner had warned us about at one of our many meetings. She was losing control of her bodily functions. Stephanie rolled over in bed and felt her underpants. "Mommy, I peed to bed. I didn't mean to, Mommy. I'm sorry." She saw me standing over her.

"It's okay, sweetheart. I'll get you some dry clothes." In an emotional stupor, I gathered the clean clothes and bed linens.

Back in a dry, warm bed, I held Stephanie close, listening to the rhythmic ticking of the orange and white *Garfield the cat* clock hanging on the wall next to the dresser. The tail wagging back and forth moved the large brown eyes from side to side, counting off the seconds, the minutes, the hours, just another reminder that we were running out of time.

I called Dr. Turner the next morning and told him what had happened. I could hear the concern in his voice. He wanted to see Stephanie.

He sat at his desk in his dark green cardigan sweater, his gray and green striped tie slightly askew, flipping through the various reports of the day's tests. He frowned, rubbed his chin, and cleared his throat. "Have Stephanie at the hospital by twelve-thirty on Wednesday, February nineteenth." He glanced at us and then fastened his eyes on Stephanie.

I heard a long, heavy sigh come from Ronnie, and I felt the harsh, sharp intake of my own breath. We would have one more week with Stephanie at home before the operation.

Just one week. Always, always it was *time*. Too much. Too little. Too long. Too short.

All week we watched Stephanie for signs of loss of her bodily functions. Nothing. I had covered her mattress with a rubber sheet just in case.

But, while she wasn't wetting her bed, she was lethargic and her speech was slowed. Maybe a week was too long.

Should I call Dr. Turner? Probably not.

But, what if . . . I wouldn't allow myself to think beyond the *if*.

Maybe a week wasn't long enough. Could we hold her enough? Could we kiss her enough? Could we talk to her enough? Could we love her enough?

How much was *enough*?

The week dragged on. The week flew by in a blur.

Finally, it was time to go.

I lingered by the back door, looked around the kitchen, checked for any appliance that could possibly have been left on accidentally, ran back upstairs to check the bedrooms one last time, stopped by Stephanie's room, sat down on her bed and cried. What would our little girl be like the next time she came into her bedroom? The doctors had assured us that the removal of that particular part of the brain wouldn't have any major impact on her abilities or her personality. I wanted to believe them, but I couldn't imagine that she could ever be the same with part of her brain missing.

As the doubts and fears crept through my mind, I was gripped by a sudden incapacitating terror. What if I hadn't gleaned and stored enough memories? What if our little girl wasn't the same when she came home and I couldn't capture her loving, vibrant personality in my mind? What if stepping out our back door today changed our lives forever?

I didn't want to take the next step. Once we arrived at the hospital, we would have no control over what was going to happen to Stephanie. Nothing would ever be the same.

My memory bank would hold memories that weren't so happy.

I straightened the caricatures above the bed. I tried to shut the closet door. I looked at the Garfield clock.

Stephanie was wheeled into room 825 on the Oncology floor. A constant swarm of doctors and nurses rushed in and out.

Dr. Oliver, with his team of oncology surgeons trailing behind him, explained that we would be given progress reports every two hours of the eight hour operation.

"Do you have any questions for me?" He folded his arms across his chest and smiled like he had just given the latest update on a flight schedule. Flight was on my mind. I wanted to take Stephanie and flee.

As the young anesthesiologist, who had come into the room to explain his part in the operation, was leaving, he said, "Mrs. Black, you can stay with Stephanie until the very last minute. I know she'll be frightened and want you there, so you don't have to leave until she's sound asleep." He smiled tenderly.

"You have a good night." He shook hands with Ronnie and me and walked out of the room.

Have a good night? How do you have a good night when your child is facing the removal of part of her brain? How do you have a good night when you're thinking it might be her last night?

Have a good night? It would be a sleepless night, not a good night.

Ronnie stood by the bed holding Stephanie's hand. The muscles and veins in his neck were constricting as he swallowed, trying to keep from crying. It was time to say good-bye. "Daddy's coming back in the morning, Babe. I love you." He bent and kissed her cheek, the tears threatening to break free.

After Ronnie was gone, I sat in the chair by the window. I watched the clock. Time was going too slow. Time was going too fast.

I listened to the dissonance of the traffic streaming by below. I listened to the hum and vibration of the heating unit in the room. I listened to Stephanie's even, steady breathing as she slept.

I felt the tremor in the floor when the elevator doors opened and shut. I felt the pulsing of the machine that was connected to Stephanie's arm. I felt the thudding of my heart.

More than anything, I felt the loss of life as we had known it.

Tumor. Malignant. Inoperable. Those fateful words had started a landslide of activity that had changed our lives. And now the operation. Though taking a portion of Stephanie's brain out was intended to *buy* us *time*, it was one more step towards the inevitable.

I sat in the chair all night watching Stephanie sleep. Should we have told her that she was going to have an operation? What should I say to her in the morning when they come to take her downstairs?

Stephanie groaned.

I had been deep in thought, staring out the window, as the light began to filter into the room. It wasn't daybreak yet, but the sky was getting brighter. Now I jumped at the strange sound.

"Oh, sweetheart, I didn't know that you were awake." I hurried to the side of the bed. I stared at her face. Her eyes were closed. She was groaning in her sleep.

"Do you have to go to the bathroom, honey?" I rubbed her arm and stroked her face. She opened her eyes. She tried to talk, but the sound was garbled and weak.

"Oh, no." I bent over the bed and cradled her in my arms.

The door swung open and a nurse came in holding a tray with medications. "Well, I didn't know you two were awake. What are you doing up so early? It's just five o'clock." She placed her tray on Stephanie's bedside table.

"Stephanie's trying to talk to me, but she can't form the words. There's something wrong." I began to shiver. What was happening?

She bent over the bed and did a cursory examination, then pressed a button, summoning another nurse. When the nurse rushed in, she instructed her to get the floor doctor and contact Dr. Turner.

When the doctor arrived, they busied themselves checking Stephanie's vital signs. I paced the floor. They gently shook her, trying to get a response. I paced the floor. More nurses and aides came into the room. They bathed Stephanie and changed her bed. I paced the floor. They rechecked Stephanie's vital signs. I paced the floor. They tried to prop her up against her pillows. She slid to one side. I paced the floor. Time was going too slow. Where was Dr. Turner?

Finally, I heard the soft squish of his shoes coming down the hallway.

With the words tumbling out of my mouth, I told him that she was drowsy and lethargic, that she had wet her pants, that she couldn't hold herself up in the bed, and that she was acting like she was already sedated. "I don't have a good feeling about this," I concluded. I was in a frenzied state.

He held Stephanie's eyes open with one hand and waved the flashlight back and forth with the other hand. He straightened and turned towards me. I could see the concern in his eyes. "I've contacted Dr. Oliver. We'll proceed as quickly as we can."

Ronnie, Robyn and Jennifer arrived in time to say good-bye to Stephanie before they wheeled her away. Like me, the girls tried to cover up their emotions with humor. They told her she was lucky that she was going to have a nice long sleep, and it wasn't fair because they had to get up early to come to the hospital. Then, unable to avoid the gravity of the situation any longer, each one held her hand, mumbled words of encouragement, reminded her that George would be waiting for her, kissed her, told her they loved her, and fought back tears.

It didn't matter what they said or did. Stephanie did not respond. Her eyes opened and closed, but did not focus. Her mouth moved, but no words came out. Confusion shrouded their faces. What had happened since they had last seen her?

Ronnie stood silently stroking Stephanie's forehead. Again, I could see the muscles and veins in his neck constricting. He leaned down, kissed her cheek and in a strained, quavering voice said, "I love you, Babe. And don't you worry; when you wake up we'll be right there."

I was hustled into a room where I was told to don the suit that was hanging from a hook. It didn't look like a *bunny suit* to me, as the anesthesiologist had described. When I had put everything on, I looked like an astronaut complete with the headgear. The suit, shoes, gloves, and helmet-like hat were all white.

My worry over what Stephanie's reaction would be when she saw me would not be an issue. She was groggy and incoherent. She seemed unaware that I was even there. I grasped her tiny hand in mine and held it to my lips. I kissed her, caressed her, and told her over and over how much I loved her.

We sat in the black vinyl chairs that lined the walls of the waiting room, trying not to notice the other people sitting across from us. I had picked up some sports magazines for Ronnie and me. I noticed that Robyn was reading a home decorating magazine. Was she getting some ideas for her new house? Jennifer was reading a fashion magazine. Jennifer always looked *put—together*. She didn't get her fashion sense from me. I realized that I had been absent-mindedly flipping through the pages of my magazine, while I watched Ronnie and the girls, unable to concentrate long enough to read anything. Ronnie had put his magazine down and was working a crossword puzzle. Robyn was standing at the large windows that looked out into the hallway, staring straight ahead. Jennifer crossed and uncrossed her legs, her magazine still open to the first page.

We fidgeted. What time was it now? We paced. Just nine-thirty? Time was going too slow. We pretended to read.

Now I looked directly at the people across from us. They were fidgeting. They were pacing. They were pretending to read.

I wondered what was wrong with their loved one. How long would their operation take? Were they as frightened as we were? Would they drink the coffee from the large urn that sat on a table in the corner?

We fidgeted. We paced. We pretended to read. We talked occasionally, quietly, about mundane things, never about what was happening in the operating room. We got lost in our own thoughts. We watched the clock.

What time was it now? Just ten-thirty? Time was going too slow.

We were promised an update every two hours, so we tensed every time the phone rang, disappointed when the call wasn't for us. When the call was for us, we took the phone, filled with anxiety. The nurse explained where they were in the process, what would be happening next, and assured us that Stephanie was doing fine.

Lunch time came and went. We didn't eat. No one wanted to leave the room for that long. We drank water and soda. We dashed to the bathroom, one at a time.

We sat in our chairs, exhausted from doing nothing. We stretched our legs. We yawned, though we couldn't have slept.

What time was it now?

As the nurse led us into the intensive care unit, my heart lurched. Stephanie was covered with a white sheet pulled up to her chin, and her head was swathed in white bandages with a drainage tube coming out of her head. The machines that stood at the side of her bed were thumping, hissing, beeping and pulsing. The wires that were attached to the machines were protruding from various parts of her body.

I couldn't stop shivering. I wanted to touch her, but I was afraid that I would cause an alarm to go off. I wanted to hold her, but she looked too fragile. I wanted to assure her that we were all here waiting for her to wake up. I stared at Dr. Oliver. "So, she's going to be okay?" My voice came out in a whisper.

"She came through the operation very well. Of course, we'll be monitoring her closely, but we don't expect any problems. She has already been able to follow commands when we ask her to move her toes or fingers."

At that very moment, Stephanie began twitching and shaking. She was having a seizure. "Oh, no." Instinctively, I rushed to hold her.

"She's okay. It's not unusual for a patient to have a seizure after having this type operation." He scanned all of the numbers appearing on her numerous machines. "She's doing fine. Her vitals are good. She's going to be sleeping for quite awhile, so I suggest you get something to eat and return a little later."

We were emotionally drained, but at the same time, we were in a festive mood. Stephanie had come through the operation without any complications. We would eat dinner at the lodge restaurant. Our dinner would be served to us. No cafeteria food, no sandwich from a machine, no pack of crackers tonight.

That night, I lay in bed staring at the ceiling. Though I had enjoyed dinner, my mind never left Stephanie, lying in the intensive care unit, all hooked up and bandaged. Morning couldn't come soon enough.

I sat on the edge of the bed watching the clock. The nurse had said we shouldn't call before seven-thirty. As the minute hand reached the six at the bottom of the clock face, I dialed the hospital number.

"Stephanie had a reasonably good night, but she did keep calling for you. I told her you'd be here soon." The nurse's report tore at my heart.

"Why wasn't I there? Why didn't I stay with her?" I clutched the pillow and cried.

Ronnie, sitting beside me, said, "You weren't there because they wouldn't allow you to be there. They told you we couldn't see her through the night."

What he said was true. They did tell us that we weren't allowed to be in the room with Stephanie during the night, but knowing that didn't take away the hollow, sinking feeling that permeated my whole body.

I clutched her tiny hand and pressed it to my mask-covered lips. Her blue eyes fastened on me. "I wanted you to sleep with me last night." Her voice was strained and weak. Her eyes were sad.

My heart leaped inside my shaking body.

Tears slipped down my face, spreading over the mask that covered my nose and mouth. "Oh, my Special Angel, I wanted to sleep with you, but they wouldn't let me. I would have been here if I could have my baby doll."

How would she ever understand? I had always stayed with her and slept with her in all of her other hospital stays. My heart ached at the thought of her being frightened and alone.

I peered into her eyes. She was staring straight ahead. Her eyes were glazed over. What was wrong? One statement to me and now her eyes weren't focusing.

Ronnie and I both attempted to engage her in conversation. She never responded. We asked questions, gave her commands. No response.

She closed her eyes and appeared to go to sleep. I asked the nurse if there was something wrong. I felt that burning sensation in my stomach again.

"Dr. Oliver is due to come in at any minute." She glanced at the machines that were attached to Stephanie.

We stood by her bedside. She opened her eyes. They were still glazed over. She appeared to be looking through us, not at us. Her skin was extremely pale. Nervously, we waited for Dr. Oliver.

"Stephanie's not responding to questions or commands. Is there something wrong with her? Don't you think she looks pale?" I assailed him with questions the minute he appeared in the room.

Ignoring me, he read the chart, checked the machines, looked in Stephanie's eyes with the flashlight, and examined the connections leading from the machines and into Stephanie.

"She's doing fine." He sighed, and continued, as though explaining to a child, "She has just undergone an eight hour operation and had a portion of her brain removed. She's tired. She needs her rest and her sleep." He smiled, reassuringly. "Dr. Turner and I will stop by her room later today."

I couldn't help it: No matter how reassuring he was, when I looked at Stephanie, I couldn't believe him.

By eleven o'clock, Stephanie was settled into room 809, Jennifer had arrived with her boyfriend, Jeff, and we started our vigil. We talked, watched television, read magazines, and periodically stood by Stephanie's bed trying to get her to respond to us. Stephanie slept.

As promised, Dr. Turner and Dr. Oliver arrived shortly after noon. Greeting us with enthusiasm, they both checked her eyes and her tubes.

"Well, our girl is doing just fine. She really came through the operation well." Dr. Turner's voice was filled with elation.

I hesitated. How do I tell a doctor that I disagree with him when he has all of the medical knowledge and equipment, and all I have is my mother's intuition?

"Yes, but, she just sleeps. We can't get her to say anything. And, she doesn't look good. She's so pale. She's too lethargic." I knew that Dr. Oliver had answered my questions earlier, but I wanted to see how Dr. Turner reacted.

"Dr. Oliver told me of your concern, but everything seems to be fine. We're monitoring her closely. If there's any change, we'll know about it." His smile was both encouraging and understanding.

But, as the afternoon wore on, I couldn't shake the fear that was gripping me. Stephanie was still sleeping. The nurse had brought in some Jell-O and liquids with instructions to wake Stephanie and feed her as much as we could possibly get into her.

We stroked her. We shook her. We coaxed her. We pleaded with her. We tried to feed her without her cooperation. We forced a few bites of Jell-O into her mouth. She coughed. We stopped forcing food on her, afraid she would choke. She slept on.

When the nurse came in on one of her occasional visits, I pointed at the tray that still held Stephanie's Jell-O. "We tried everything we could think of, but we can't get Stephanie to wake up and eat. The doctors keep saying that she's fine, but, quite frankly, we don't see it that way." My voice was rising. Panic was overtaking me.

She picked up the flashlight, looked in Stephanie's eyes, and said that she would have some of Dr. Oliver's assistants stop by and check on Stephanie, but everything appeared to be just fine.

We were surrounded by doctors, nurses, technicians, and the finest medical equipment available. Why couldn't I relax? What was I afraid of? Hadn't we been assured and reassured that everything was okay?

Stephanie's sleep was getting deeper and deeper. I could distinguish the difference in her breathing. Shouldn't the anesthesia be wearing off? Shouldn't she be caught up on her rest and sleep? Shouldn't her color be better twenty-four hours after her operation? Shouldn't she be rousing from her sleep?

Though the doctors kept reassuring us that Stephanie was doing fine, Ronnie was hesitating to leave because he knew that I was nervous and upset. "I can stay if you want. I can stay at the lodge for one more night." He was asking for my approval.

But I was beginning to feel foolish. Of course, he didn't need to stay one more night. "No, you go on home. We'll be fine, and we'll see you in the morning."

"Are you sure?"

"Yes, I'm sure."

But, I wasn't.

With some misgivings, he, Jennifer, and Jeff said good-bye, promising Stephanie that they would be back tomorrow, and glancing back as they walked out the door. I knew they were as distraught and as unsure as I was.

I glanced at the clock: Four-forty-five. They would get home in time for dinner. I paced the floor, stood by the bed and held Stephanie's frail hand, sat by the window, paged through a magazine. I listened to Stephanie's breathing getting increasingly heavier and louder.

I glanced at the clock: Five-fifteen. They would be halfway home, maybe, if traffic wasn't heavy. I paced the floor, stood by the bed and pressed Stephanie's pale hand against my lips, flipped TV channels, paged through another magazine. I listened to Stephanie's breathing becoming deeper and noisier.

I glanced at the clock: Five-fifty. They should be home by now or at least close to home. Where was the nurse? She hadn't been in since Ronnie left. Didn't one of Dr. Oliver's assistants order a CAT scan? Why hadn't they come to get Stephanie?

Stephanie's breathing was now a deep, loud, guttural sound. It wasn't a snore. She wasn't asleep. No way was she in a natural sleep. I clutched her hand to my face. I sobbed. "Oh, God, please help me. What should I do?" I had tried desperately to get someone, anyone, to recognize what I felt and knew in my heart, but to no avail. What more *could I* do?

My blood was pounding inside of my head. I pressed the buzzer for the nurse. Now, I was panic-stricken. "Answer," I shouted to the empty room.

The door swung open. "What can I do . . . ?"

I cut her off in mid-sentence. "There's something wrong with Stephanie. And don't tell me she's okay. She's not." I shouted at her as I stood by Stephanie's side, willing her to see what I was seeing and knowing.

She snatched up the flashlight and pointed the light into Stephanie's eyes, then she smashed a button at the head of the bed and shouted "Code Blue! Code Blue! Code Blue!"

The door flew open with a barrage of nurses and doctors, all shouting orders and directions, scurrying and scampering around the bed, dashing back out the door pushing Stephanie in her bed down the hallway.

"Oh no, oh no, oh God, no," I kept repeating. As I ran to the door, trying to follow the throng of people hustling Stephanie away, I saw Dr. Oliver sprinting toward them. He grabbed a corner of the bed and pushed with the rest of them.

Standing in the doorway, I was shrieking, "Stephanie! Stephanie!" Where were they taking her? What was happening to her? What should I do? I started to run after them.

"What's happening, Carole? What's going on?" Helen and Dominic were standing in my way. Where did they come from? Why were they here?

"It's Stephanie. The nurse was shouting Code Blue. She kept shouting Code Blue. They just grabbed her bed and . . . I don't know where . . . I've got to find her. I kept telling them . . . . I knew she wasn't as good today as . . . . I've got to find her. She'll be scared if I'm not there." I was screaming, rambling and sobbing. My whole body was trembling. I had to get to Stephanie. I shoved Helen aside, but Dominic grabbed me.

"Carole, listen to me. Where's Ronnie?"

"I've got to . . . She'll think I . . . She needs me." Still shouting, with tears coursing down my cheeks, I struggled to free myself. I had to follow Stephanie.

"Carole, listen to me. Did Ronnie go home? Who was with him?" Helen was grasping my shoulders and shaking me.

Trying to subdue the sobs that were wracking my body, I gasped, "Yes, yes, he's gone . . . he's with Jennifer and . . . and . . . Jeff." I was fighting to control myself, but my mind was focused on Stephanie. Where did they take her?

At some point we were led to a room down the hall where we were told to wait. I slumped into a chair. I was physically and emotionally exhausted, and I was paralyzed with fear. I could no longer cry. I could no longer pray. I could no longer feel.

After a while, Dr. Turner, Dr. Oliver, and one of his assistants, came into the room. They pulled up chairs and surrounded me, still slumped in my chair, staring into space, barren of all emotion.

"Mrs. Black," Dr. Oliver began, scrutinizing my face. Was I listening? "Stephanie's condition is critical. There is fluid build-up inside her skull, which caused her brain to be pushed down toward the brain stem. We are working to get her stabilized, but I can't promise you anything. Do you understand?" He paused. "If you haven't contacted the rest of your family, you need to do it now." He paused. Awkwardly, he reached over and touched my arm.

I sat, still staring into space, my mind riveted on his words. *Critical . . . fluid build up . . . brain stem . . . get stabilized . . . can't promise . . . understand . . . contact family . . . do it now . . .*

"Can I see her?"

"It would be best if you could wait for another hour or so. We're still working on her." He paused. "Aggressively," he added.

I folded my arms across my body and rocked back and forth. Ronnie and the girls would be here soon.

Helen, Dominic, and I sat in the quiet of the waiting room.

Frightened and exhausted, my voice trembled, as I asked, "Helen, why did you come down this evening?" I was glad that she and Dominic were here, but I wondered why, since I had phoned and assured her that Stephanie had come through the operation without any problems.

Helen slid forward in her chair, reached over and held my hand. "I had this funny feeling all day long, like something was wrong. I kept thinking that maybe you needed me. So, when Dominic came home, he took one look at me and said, 'you want to go to the hospital, don't you?' I said yes and here we are. I don't know how I knew, but I just knew." She pulled me into her arms and hugged me, tears filling her eyes.

I hugged her back as tears streamed down my face. I was feeling again.

What time was it? Why weren't Ronnie and the girls here? The minutes seemed like hours.

"Excuse me, Mrs. Black?" I looked up and saw a man clad in black. "I'm the hospital chaplain. I understand that your daughter is very ill. I want you to know how sorry I am, and if it will help, I'd like to sit with you for awhile." His voice was filled with compassion as he reached to touch my shoulder.

Immediately, tears trickled down my face. It was worse than the doctors had indicated. Stephanie wasn't going to make it. There wasn't any hope. There wasn't going to be any attempt to stabilize her. They were just waiting for her to die. Why else would the chaplain be here? How would he know to come to me? The doctors sent him. Why would the doctors send a chaplain to me if they weren't expecting Stephanie to die? Why should I trust anything that any of the doctors said to me? All day long they told me Stephanie was doing just fine. All day long I knew she wasn't. Stephanie was dying. I curled into a ball and sobbed.

"I can't talk to you now," I mumbled between sobs.

"You don't have to talk to me. I'll talk to you, or I'll just sit here with you." The empathy clearly showed in his voice. "Could we pray together?"

I nodded.

After a while, the chaplain suggested we take a walk to the chapel. As we started down the hallway, Ronnie and Jennifer appeared around the corner.

"Oh, God, no," Ronnie shouted. He ran towards me, tears streaming down his face. "Oh no, oh no," he kept repeating, as he reached for me.

All of a sudden, it hit me: He thought Stephanie had died. Why else would I be with the chaplain?

"No, no, she's okay. She's really bad, but she's . . . he's just with me." I babbled on, trying to calm him.

Jennifer stood by, tears streaming down her face. Was I telling the truth? Her Aunt Helen wrapped her arms around her, reassuring her that Stephanie was still alive. "She's okay. She's having a rough time, but she's still here."

We walked back to the waiting room. Robyn had arrived and was waiting for us.

We sat huddled together, hugging, holding hands, each of us lost in our own thoughts.

Before long, the waiting room was filled with my sisters, brothers, brothers-in-law, and sisters-in-law. Helen had sneaked away and called Janice, who had spread the word and now they were here to support us.

Sometime after midnight, Dr. Turner came into the waiting room. He stopped and looked, somewhat surprised. "They're all family," I explained.

He smiled and nodded. "Stephanie is stabilized. However, if you could wait until morning to see her, it would be best for her. I assure you, she is responding to what we're doing, but it is a very busy place right now, and will be for a few more hours."

Ronnie and I looked at him in disbelief. We'd been waiting for hours to see her. If we didn't see her now, would we ever see her alive again?

And I needed to be with her now. *'I wanted you to sleep with me last night'* echoed inside my head.

Jennifer, Robyn, Ronnie and I sat in the waiting room all night, waiting for news, anxiously watching the hallway for a doctor or nurse to come in and give us an update, but relieved when no one showed up.

As the morning light filtered through the blinds, Dr. Turner strode into the waiting room. "Good morning. Did you get any rest sitting here?"

I knew he was trying to be kind, but I wanted to hear about Stephanie. "No, I don't think we rested very well, but . . ." My voice trailed off. What else was there to say? I wasn't interested in small talk.

"As we told you last night, Stephanie's condition is critical, but her chances have improved because she made it through the night. However, we will have to keep her in intensive care. *Her chances have improved . . . Her chances have improved . . . Her chances have improved . . .*

He went on talking, but all I heard was . . . *her chances have improved . . .*

"Can we see her now?" I stood, waiting for his okay.

"Yes, all of you can go in, but you won't be able to stay long. And . . . don't expect her to be able to respond to you. Not yet." He shifted his feet and studied his hands as he prepared us for disappointment.

It was the same cold, white, sterile room that we had entered yesterday, but, somehow, it seemed to be even colder than before. And it had an air of foreboding. I kept picturing the morgues that I had seen on TV programs. I shook my head, trying to dislodge that horrifying image.

There were more tubes protruding from Stephanie than there had been the day of her operation, and the noises persisted. Each thump, hiss, beep, and pulse coursed through my body. They seemed to be counting off the seconds, minutes, hours and days. How many did we have left?

Stephanie's feet were sticking out from under the sheet that draped her body. I reached over and covered the foot closest to me with my hand. It was frigid and lifeless. I touched her other foot. It too was bitter cold. I began to panic. If I didn't hear the machines working to keep Stephanie alive, I would have sworn she was dead. If her feet were that cold, the rest of her body was probably cold too.

"Stephanie's feet are too cold. Shouldn't she have something on her feet? Don't you have some sort of sock or booty to put on her?"

I repeated myself as nurses and technicians hurried in and out of the room. Finally, a nurse appeared with a pair of white socks. Why did everything have to be white?

We stood talking to Stephanie, soothing her, reassuring her, and watching for some response. A twitch? A blink? A jerk?

Nothing.

The human body experiences a powerful gravitational pull in the direction of hope. That is why the patient's hopes are the physician's secret weapon. They are the hidden ingredients in any prescription.

Norman Cousins

Jennifer and Robyn returned home, and Ronnie and I returned to the lodge. Each day we visited Stephanie, retreating to the waiting room when our time was up, going back into the ICU when we were allowed. Each day the doctors gave us an update. Each day we called Robyn and Jennifer. Each day we called Helen, and she spread the latest information to the rest of the family. Each day we saw a slight improvement in Stephanie's condition. She was twitching. She was blinking. She did occasionally jerk.

And, finally, after twelve days, Stephanie was moved into her own room, far from being the little girl that we brought into the hospital just over two weeks ago, but better than she had been the day after the operation.

What is it they say about all things being relative? How could we possibly look at Stephanie and think that she was better? She was still hooked up to all of her machines. She still required constant and vigilant care. She was only semi-conscious. But, she was out of the ICU. Wasn't that better?

Each day after Stephanie was moved from the ICU, we saw small improvements. She began to awaken and look around. She responded to commands, and made eye contact with us. She pointed to the right person when we asked her to identify us.

For the first time in almost a month, I was having positive thoughts and feelings. Maybe we would have more time with Stephanie than we had anticipated before the operation.

We? Who was I thinking about when I thought *we*? Ronnie? Robyn?

Jennifer? I realized that I was thinking about *me*, not *we*. I didn't want to lose Stephanie, not for her sake, or anybody else's sake, but for my own. I wasn't thinking about the pain and suffering that Stephanie was going through to achieve even the slightest improvement, let alone a complete recovery. I wasn't thinking about the pain, hurt, or pressure that anybody else in the family was experiencing. I was thinking about how happy *I* would be to have her home to take care of and love. Of course, it hurt me deeply to see Stephanie suffer, but, I admitted, I was willing to have her go through whatever was necessary to get her back.

When I acknowledged to myself the lengths to which I would go to keep Stephanie alive, essentially for my own needs, I was ashamed and surprised at my selfishness.

From the day that I made that startling revelation, I changed my prayers. I prayed for *Stephanie's* well-being, peace, and comfort. I didn't become wholly unselfish, but I was trying.

Shortly after the improvements began, I started to notice small indicators that, perhaps, Stephanie was beginning to regress slightly. Stop, I told myself. She's doing fine.

Could it be that I spent too much time with her? Could it be that I was expecting too much too soon? Could it be that she had reached a plateau? No, it wasn't a plateau, it was regression. Though she hadn't been talking, she was communicating with head nods, smiles, kisses, pointing, squeezing our fingers, making eye contact, and just generally following commands.

Now, she stared into space, barely moved her head, had to be prompted several times to respond to any command, and seemed listless.

My charred and ash-strewn stomach was building a new fire.

I told Dr. Turner what I was observing, and he responded immediately. He examined her thoroughly, shook his head, sighed heavily, and left the room.

When he returned, I knew it wasn't good news. His face was pale and his voice was strained. "There's been a mistake made in Stephanie's medications." He bowed his head and then rubbed his temple, his eyes squinting, like he was trying to get rid of a painful memory. "Her steroids have, inadvertently, been left out of her medication schedule for the past several days. Of course, we've ordered the steroids to be replaced immediately." He continued rubbing his temple.

I stood staring at him in astonishment. How could somebody inadvertently, or any other way, leave the steroids out of Stephanie's meds? I didn't know what to say. What could I say? I walked to the bed, cradled Stephanie in my arms, and cried.

In less than another week, they collapsed her lung while putting in a central line for medications, and she developed a blood clot in her leg. Then, when a young, overweight nurse lumbered into the room carrying a tray of medications, took one look at all of Stephanie's machines, fingered the wires and tubes, and exclaimed, "Boy, how do you know which tube gets what? You could easily put the wrong stuff into a tube if you weren't careful. Now, let me see. What goes where?" I couldn't contain myself any longer. I snapped.

I rushed out to the nurses' station. "Somebody get in there right away. She doesn't know what she's doing. She admitted she could easily put the wrong *stuff*, as she called it, into the wrong tube." I was pointing in the direction of Stephanie's room, my heart pounding wildly. "I want her out of there, and I don't want to see her in Stephanie's room again." My hands were shaking, and my head was throbbing. How much more would Stephanie have to go through? It seemed endless.

I was numb. I didn't sleep. I didn't eat. I couldn't leave Stephanie's bedside. What would happen to her if I wasn't there to watch their every move?

When steroids were reinserted into Stephanie's medical regimen, she again began to respond and improve. With guarded optimism I began to relax.

Working hard to speed Stephanie's recovery, I spent my days playing Stephanie's Kenny Rogers and Sunday school music tapes, singing along with them, encouraging her to sing with me, and then starting all over again when the tapes ran out. Tiring of the tapes, I would talk to Stephanie incessantly. I reminded her that George loved her and needed her to get better so she could take care of him. I told her stories that she knew by heart but still loved to hear. I kissed her cheeks, rubbed her arms and legs, stroked her head, patted her hands, and nuzzled her neck. I did everything I could to stimulate all of her senses.

The nurses' aides gave Stephanie her bath, rubbed her body with lotion, cleaned her mouth, and combed her hair. They were all good to Stephanie, but Lydia was special.

With her sparkling brown eyes, her ebony skin, and an affectionate smile that spread over her round face and lit up the room, Lydia approached her work like it was a privilege to be a part of her patients' lives. She more than bathed Stephanie. She caressed her tender skin with the cloth, gently patted her dry, and massaged and stroked her body with lotion, all the time talking to Stephanie about her beautiful eyes, her thick, lustrous hair, her choice in music, the weather, and, most importantly, the need for her to awaken and get better. She ended every session with a hug, a kiss on the cheek, and a murmured promise that she would see her later.

It was clear that Lydia had fallen in love with Stephanie, and I had fallen in love with Lydia for the way she treated Stephanie.

As Stephanie improved, she made eye contact, lifted her arms, pointed with her fingers, smiled, nodded in response to questions, and puckered up when asked for a kiss. She did not talk, but she did communicate.

When Stephanie was comatose, they had inserted a feeding tube, which would stay intact, since she couldn't swallow without the possibility of the food going into her lungs. This created another site open to infection, which, of course, happened. The tube area became inflamed and was treated with a bacterial cream and an antibiotic medication fed through her tube. Then she developed a staph infection which appeared over her back and buttocks.

Nothing that happened to her surprised, frightened, or enraged me anymore. I accepted it all as part of our lives. While both of these infections were bothersome, and somewhat painful, they did not compromise her improvement. She was, I thought, on the road to recovery.

While Stephanie was receiving physical and occupational therapy at the hospital, it was decided that she was ready for more intensive therapy that was available at a nearby institution. We were so excited. One more step towards getting Stephanie home. She would be moved on March eighteenth where her therapies would be intensified in difficulty and duration.

3/18/92—Moving day. Wonderful responses from Steph—smiles, squeezing of hand, pointing of finger, eyes REALLY clear—almost looks like "old" Steph—

I set the journal aside. The *old* Steph? I desperately wanted to remember the *old Steph*. I closed my eyes and pictured the times that she would pretend to be a dog, rubbing herself against my leg, barking and panting when I scratched her head and called her *Sparky*.

Stephanie had fallen asleep again and, as I stood gazing at her face, I thought of her favorite love game. Gently, as I recited the words, *I love this and this* . . . I ran my fingers down her cheeks, circling her eyes, her nose, her mouth, and when I reached the curve of her neck, I finished, . . . *and all of this*. I remembered how she would squirm and giggle, "Mommy, Mommy, it tickles, it tickles." Then, grabbing my hands, she would beg, "Let's do it again."

I glanced at the clock. It wouldn't be long now. I had packed up our few belongings, and we were waiting for our escort.

The rooms in this institution were slightly smaller than the rooms in the hospital, so it was a little harder to squeeze my cot into a corner, which meant that the chair had to be removed. I would miss my chair. At the hospital, when Stephanie was sleeping, and I tired and could no longer stand by her bed and sing and talk to her, I would sit in the chair by the window and watch her. Now I would have to sit on the cot and stretch my neck to see over the bottom of her bed.

As I positioned the tape recorder, the tapes, George and the many small things that would make this room ours, I wondered if this would be the first day of a long and arduous journey. I wanted to believe that the end result would be worth every twist, turn, stretch, pull, bend, manipulation, rotation, massage, and physical and mental probing that Stephanie would encounter and endure.

As it was in the hospital, the days in the institution all seemed to run together. The only way to tell one day from the next was by the time of day that Ronnie and the girls came, and when other people visited. Their arrivals and departures were dependent on what was going on in their lives outside of the hospital.

For Stephanie and me? Nothing changed. Occasionally, our routine was disrupted by seizures, a need for tests, a lack of response, an increase in response, a discussion on which direction future treatments should take. Gradually, even they became routine.

And time? Time was marked by routine. Time was marked by Stephanie's responses. Time was marked by Stephanie's lack of responses. Time was marked by Stephanie's need for treatment. Time was marked by doctors' decisions. In our daily routine, time was of no importance.

For our future? Time was marked by how much we had left and how much we could buy.

Thursday, Friday and Saturday of the first week in her new surroundings, Stephanie was non-responsive and slept most of the day. Was she over-medicated, or was there something else going on? I was weak with fear and trepidation, and I was mentally, emotionally and physically exhausted. So, I decided, I wouldn't allow myself to think. I wouldn't worry. I wouldn't react to anything that was, or wasn't, happening. I wouldn't question every move that the doctors and nurses made. I wouldn't allow that fire to take control in the pit of my stomach.

I tried, I really tried, but I couldn't take my eyes off Stephanie. I couldn't stop watching for responses and trying to interpret them. I couldn't allow the doctors and nurses to attend to Stephanie without watching their every move. I couldn't stop stimulating Stephanie's senses. I couldn't stop encouraging and beseeching Stephanie to respond.

Already, it was Thursday, March 26th, Ronnie was gone for the evening, Stephanie was settled in for the night, well, settled in until they came back to turn her, or medicate her, or change her diaper, or whatever else was part of the routine. I sat on my cot and read my journal entries for the last several days.

3/23—Monday—pretty good day. Responses : hearing aid beeped, reached hand up to silence it; Smiled; Squeezed my hand; Head nod to "Do you want Daddy to bring new batteries for your tape player?" ; Puckered to kiss me. P.T.—leg and foot splints on, off, bend, twist, stretch. Arms stretched, turned, lifted, massaged—not Stephanie's favorite time of day

Feet are swollen? What's going on? Mini-seizures at 7:15 and 7:55 in the morning. Why is Stephanie having seizures every day after they raised her Tegretol level?

3/24—Tuesday—Good day. Responses: Nodded yes to "Can you hear me?"; "Where's Mommy?" pointed finger at me; Opened mouth on command; When asked, "Do you like this song?" nodded yes; Relaxed arm upon command; Pointed at me when asked, "Who loves you?" ; Smiled twice when requested; Smiled for O.T. Kristin; Kristin asked, "Do you like to sit up?" Nodded yes; Nodded yes, when Kristin asked, "I'm going to give you a break, is that okay?"

3/25—Wednesday—Responses: Smiles; pointed to me when asked "Who loves you?"; Squeezed my hand; Said "Ow" when Cheryl stretched her legs.

3/26—Thursday—Responses: Opened mouth on command; stopped biting tooth cleaning stick on command; showed teeth on command; three smiles; pointed to me with thumb; turned head on own when P.T. Cheryl caused her pain; turned head on own when aide washed her face.

I closed the journal, stretched out on my cot, my arms behind my head, and reflected on the responses that I had listed in my entries. Despite the series of mini-seizures, I was pleased with what I had recorded. Each response was a bit, a tad, a morsel, a speck, a crumb of hope.

Strange, I thought, wistfully, as I stared out the window at the cloud-covered sky, how effortless it is to drift into complacency and self-satisfaction when everything in your life is going well, and then how urgently you become obsessed with the minute, the obscure, the mundane, the routine, and the expected when they are no longer minute, obscure, mundane, routine, and expected.

A curved lip is no longer just a smile—it's a pathway to success; a raised hand is no longer just a move to correct an annoyance—it's the first motion used to construct a stairway to mobility; a nod of a head is no longer just an indication of agreement or acceptance—it's a measure of understanding and compliance; a squeezed hand is no longer just a calculation of pressure—it's a gesture of warmth and affection; a verbal "ow" is no longer just an expression of pain—it's an awareness of self and what is happening to you; a kiss is no longer a perfunctory action or reaction-it is the epitome of love and caring.

Never again, I promised myself, would I allow myself to drift into the thoughtless, mindless, repetitive motions of everyday life. I would appreciate and savor everybody and everything.

Though we were in a neighboring institution, Dr. Turner was still responsible for Stephanie's over-all care. He would come over and talk to us about Stephanie's progress, or lack of, and if, and when, the radiation treatments should start.

In his most recent visits, he expressed concern about the seizure activity, the dwindling responses, and the inability to stay awake. Stephanie was sleeping more and more. I was very much aware of Stephanie's regression; I had recorded everything in my journal, but I couldn't stand to hear him vocalize the very things I had been observing and writing about.

Now, as Dr. Turner entered the room, I knew the news wasn't good. I could read his pained face, his sad eyes.

"How's Stephanie doing today?"

I wanted to scream at him. *Go away! Don't talk! I don't want to hear what you have to say! Don't take my hope away! Don't make me face what I already know!* "About the same, I guess." I stroked Stephanie's arm, held her hand, and rubbed her cheek, avoiding his eyes.

"We were planning to start radiation treatments on Monday, but we have some concerns regarding the wisdom of this decision." He tugged at his tie, clasped his hands behind his back, and wrinkled his brow. "Dr. La Torra, and I feel that they, the therapists especially, can't do any more for Stephanie at this stage of her recovery, so we're considering moving her back to the hospital."

I felt my face flush with frustration and disappointment. Why couldn't they keep trying to work with her? Why couldn't they keep trying to elicit responses? Why couldn't they feel our urgency, our fear, our desperation?

"However, now that she's been moved out of the hospital, it might be very difficult to get her back in. It's possible that they'll say she needs to go to a nursing home."

They. They. They. Who were *they*? I didn't know *they,* but I resented their superiority, their apparent lack of compassion, their control over our lives.

Tears saturated my eyes, but I didn't say anything. I just kept staring at Stephanie. No one wanted her. No one cared that she was struggling for her life, or that *her time* was running out. *They* would get rid of her, their failed project, and make room for the next unsuspecting victim. Anger and bitterness engulfed my thoughts.

"Of course, we'll fight to get her back into the hospital, but you know how it is with insurance companies. They'll fight us tooth and nail." He shifted his feet and crossed his arms.

I could feel the warmth of the sun beating on my back as I continued to stand at the side of Stephanie's bed. Why was the sun shining? There was no sunshine in our lives.

His eyes remained fastened on me, but I couldn't look at him. I would cry, and that was the last thing I wanted to do. I bit my lip and straightened the sheet covering Stephanie.

"Right now, we're looking to move her back on April the 4th, if everything works out with insurance, and we'll get another CAT scan. We need to know what's going on, what's causing the seizures, the regression." He came around the bed to where I was standing. He put his hand on my shoulder and said, softly, "I promise, we'll do everything in our power to keep Stephanie with us. We'll fight for her right to get the care she needs." Abruptly, he turned and left the room.

Blindly, I made my way to the cot and collapsed, sobbing uncontrollably. I would not, could not, put Stephanie into a nursing home to whither away and die. Alone.

I couldn't stop shivering. I crawled under the blanket, covered my head and continued to cry. Pictures of neglect and abuse flashed through my mind. No one would take care of her like I would. No one would love her and nurture her like I would. No one would look after her needs like I would. No one would come to her in the middle of the night if she awakened frightened. No one. No one. No one. I would not let it happen. I could not let it happen.

For the next few days I cringed every time I saw Dr. Turner come into Stephanie's room. Did he have news? Was it good news? Was it bad news? Would the insurance company acquiesce and give Stephanie the right to get the care she needed? Would that decision then allow Stephanie to be transferred back into the oncology department at the hospital? Would all of these decisions combined keep Stephanie out of a nursing home?

On Sunday, March twenty-ninth, Dr. Turner came into Stephanie's room, smiling, but, less than enthusiastic. "I have some good news and some bad news. Theresa is making some headway with the insurance company. It looks as though *they* are at least willing to listen to our side of the story." He nodded hello to Ronnie.

I winced. There was that word again. *They.*

He continued, "However, the negotiations are not at the point where we can move Stephanie back into the hospital. But, it does look hopeful."

"So that's the good news and the bad news?" My voice was lifeless. It was getting harder and harder to get enthused about any news that came from anyone concerning Stephanie. Even good news wasn't especially good anymore. Too soon there would be news that would alter, modify, or amend the good news and, once again, we would be disillusioned.

"Well, no, . . ." he hesitated, "that was the good news. The bad news is that we have decided that we just can't begin radiation now, based on what we see happening."

Ronnie's shoulders slumped, and he sighed heavily.

I watched a bird building a nest on the corner of the window sill. Maybe there would be baby birds soon. New life.

"We need to get another CAT scan and an MRI to determine what's going on inside of Stephanie's head. You want us to be doing something to shrink the tumor; I fully understand that." He had noticed Ronnie's reaction. "But as Stephanie's doctors, we have to make sure that we're doing the right thing, and right now, we're not sure that the right thing is radiation." He glanced at us, waiting for the impact of his words to settle upon us.

I continued watching the bird build a sanctuary for new life.

He walked to the doorway, hesitated, and said, "Don't get discouraged." The soft, squeak of his footsteps echoed down the hallway.

Don't get discouraged? Stephanie had been in the hospital since February nineteenth, and now we were approaching the first of April and she was still in the hospital.

Don't get discouraged? The day after the operation Stephanie languished in her room while doctor after doctor pronounced her okay when I politely, but nervously, pointed out the many signs of failing health that were so obvious to me.

Don't get discouraged? Stephanie spent twelve traumatic days and nights in the ICU, while we wallowed in fear, petrified that she would never recover.

Don't get discouraged? Someone inadvertently omitted steroids from Stephanie's medications and she began to regress from what little progress she had made.

Don't get discouraged? Someone had punctured Stephanie's lung.

Don't get discouraged? Stephanie developed a blood clot in her leg, a staph infection over the trunk of her body, and a continual infection surrounded her feeding tube.

Don't get discouraged? Stephanie's mini-seizures continued to grow in intensity and length despite numerous changes in her medication. It was time to stop calling them *mini*.

Don't get discouraged? The precious, innocent little girl that had already suffered so much during her short lifetime was now lying in a bed with an inoperable brain tumor, barely able to respond to commands, unable to speak, eating through a tube, laboring to respond to physical and occupational therapy, and waiting for some impersonal, uncaring insurance company, clearly taking their own good time, to make a decision that would affect the rest of her life. The rest of our lives. And we had so *little time* left.

Don't get discouraged? You have to feel encouraged in order to become discouraged. I hadn't felt encouraged in a long time.

As we waited for the tests to be scheduled, I began to think about the radiation treatments. We'd already been told that Stephanie's hair would fall out, and that there would possibly be other side-effects. Fatigue? Stephanie had no energy now. Could her frail, wasting—away body take more abuse? Loss of appetite? She was being fed through a tube. They fed her how much or how little they determined that she needed.

And, because they had difficulty regulating her intake, she was bordering on obese. Skin rash? Already Stephanie's skin was a blotchy-red, with an acne-like rash all over her face, brought on by the massive doses of steroids. Nausea? Just one more malady to add to a long list.

Stephanie was no longer the petite, delicate, fair-complexioned, smooth-skinned, little girl that had come to the hospital six weeks ago. And, if they decided that she should have the radiation treatments, she would soon be bald.

When do side-effects become the norm and the norm become a thing of the past? How subtle the transition.

True to his word, Dr. Turner and Theresa had worked hard and had convinced the insurance company that Stephanie needed to be back in the hospital, not a nursing home.

We met in Dr. Turner's office. It seemed like an eternity ago that I had sat here counting floor tiles and admiring the pictures on the wall. Dr. Turner cleared his throat, leaned forward in his chair, and clasped his hands on top of his desk. "There's no easy way to tell you what we've learned from our latest tests. Stephanie's tumor is growing, it's also more diffused throughout her brain than we originally thought, and there is hemorrhaging on the left side of her brain."

Tumor is growing . . . . more diffused . . . . hemorrhaging . . . . His words pelted me like shards of sleet in a winter storm. The force of his words perforated my skin and punctured my already wounded and vulnerable heart. I no longer had the energy to fight off the impact of the cruel and pitiless words that bombarded us relentlessly and threatened to swallow us day after day. I gave in to the oppressive weight of the brutal and merciless implication of Dr. Turner's words and wept openly. Those same black tiles were unyielding in their efforts to crush the life out of me.

"I know that none of this is easy for you and your family but, again, I don't want you to get discouraged. We're doing everything we can." Dr. Turner moved from his desk and stood near our chairs, his head bowed, his eyes closed.

He spread his hands in a helpless, defeated gesture. "I'm so sorry."

Wednesday, April 1—Good amount of awake time. Pointed at me when asked "Who loves you?" Nodded head yes when asked if she wanted to go home. Nodded head yes when shown George and asked if she loved him. Smiled, nodded yes when asked if she wanted to hug me. Smiled when I reminded her of how she likes April fool's day. Spasms in both arms—then just left arm for approximately 5 minutes.

Thursday, April 2—Not much activity today. Sleeping more.

Friday, April 3—Arms twitching a lot. Arms seem tense—Wide awake at times, but no responses. Ate a bite of chocolate pudding for Kristin (trying to see if she can swallow enough to take her off of tube feeding). Stopped biting on swab used to clean mouth when asked to. Few responses to my requests. Developing blisters—don't know from what.

Saturday, April 4—not awake much—lot of seizure activity—eyes wide open, staring, breathing heavily, small arm movements

Sunday, April 5—Waking occasionally. Tensing when Edwin takes vitals.

As I read through my journal entries, I realized that Stephanie's improvements had, indeed, been few. If any.

As the days and nights passed, Stephanie slept more, her seizure activity increased, her responses decreased, and she developed a fever.

Family and friends came and went, as they had been doing since the middle of February. Stephanie slept through most of the visits, so occasionally we would leave the room and go down to the cafeteria and have something to eat. We talked about everything but Stephanie and her condition. Our emotions were too raw, too near the surface, too vulnerable to the tears that lingered just beneath the façade with which we had fortified ourselves.

Doctors and technicians came to check on her vital signs, draw blood to check levels, and discuss what was, or what wasn't, happening. And life, as we had learned to accept it, inched along in varying degrees of hope and despair.

We were planning to celebrate Jennifer's twentieth birthday, but not in Stephanie's room. We were given permission to hold the party in a large reception room at the end of the hallway. The possibility of doing something other than sit in a room surrounded by machines that stood like sentinels keeping watch over Stephanie, documenting her struggle for life, appealed to me. For the first time in a long time, I was looking forward to something. I felt the excitement building inside of me.

As I sat making a list of what we would need for the party, I could feel somebody watching me. I looked up and saw Dr. Turner standing in the doorway wearing his white coat. No, I thought. Not now. Not today. He wasn't my friendly Mr. Rogers with the cardigan sweater. The white coat was the signal that this was official. This was serious.

He reached up and adjusted the stethoscope that hung around his neck, sat on the edge of Stephanie's bed, and then placed his hand on her shoulder. "We've come to the conclusion that giving radiation treatments to Stephanie can't make her condition any worse than it is right now."

I waited. This news wasn't too bad. After all, we'd wanted to get started with radiation treatments for some time now. Why the white coat?

"Radiation treatments are our only hope at this point." His eyes were fastened on Stephanie, as he massaged her shoulder.

OUR ONLY HOPE . . . OUR ONLY HOPE . . . OUR ONLY HOPE . . . .
She was that bad off? Of course, she was that bad off. What did I expect? But still, the words burned, seared, and blazed through the protective shield that I had so carefully constructed around my emotions.

I swallowed hard, squeezed my eyes shut to hold back the tears and sat on my hands to stop the trembling. My pulse raced. I didn't respond. What could I say? I hate all things white?

After a long pause, he lifted his head. "I hear you're about to have a birthday celebration. That's good. You enjoy your time together, and I'll see you tomorrow."

He slid his hand down Stephanie's arm and grasped her tiny fingers, stroking them softly. "We'll start the radiation on Monday."

My heart was heavy and my body ached with the latest news that added to the already arduous reports that seemed to inundate us every day, but I shoved the pain of his words into the back of my mind. I would make Jennifer's birthday celebration a happy time.

The weekend seemed to go on forever, for now that they had decided to do the radiation treatments, I desperately wanted them to get started. The words *'our only hope'* beat a steady, ominous rhythm in my head and my heart.

With each passing hour, Stephanie was becoming less and less responsive; her seizures had progressed from mini to grand mall; her blisters were multiplying over her body, so they put a catheter in, trying to eliminate her lying in moisture; they were still struggling to get her Coumadin, Tegretol and thyroid medications adjusted; and her sugar levels were way too high, so they would start her on insulin shots.

By Sunday evening, as her problems continued to mount, I began to question the wisdom of giving Stephanie radiation treatments. As I sat in my familiar black vinyl chair, watching the glow of the setting sun streak through the window, making splashes of yellow and orange on the green walls, ambivalent, worrisome thoughts clamored around in my head. Shouldn't they be working to get everything else adjusted, leveled, healed, before they started her on a new treatment? How much more could her broken, battered, bruised, pain-ridden body bear? Should we say, *No, no more treatments of any kind?* Should we say, *Let her go?*

As I watched the splashes of color disappear from the wall and the gray shadows creep across the room, the ambivalent, worrisome thoughts persisted.

Should we be allowing the doctors to make all the decisions, based on their knowledge and experience? Should we be making the decisions based on our needs, our wants, our intuition? Should we be making all of the decisions, in conjunction with the doctors, based entirely on Stephanie's current condition?

The room was blanketed in darkness now. My thoughts no longer seemed important. I felt empty, worn, spent, devoid of sensation.

I sat staring into the darkness. Stephanie was sleeping, the machines were pumping, the hallways were filled with noise and chatter, but I was alone. Completely alone.

I didn't need to be alone, but I preferred it that way. The hospital social worker had been to see me several times. She had tried to get me to attend meetings with other parents who were in similar situations. Their children were dying too. I refused to attend meetings. I even refused to talk to her. She and the other parents would simply serve as reminders that Stephanie was dying. I didn't need or want them to remind me of what I already knew. No, I hadn't accepted it, but I knew it.

And, I didn't need their support, as the social worker suggested. What could they say and do that would in any way help me or Stephanie? I didn't want to see my pain mirrored in their eyes. I didn't need to know when and how they found out their child was dying. I didn't need to share with anyone how and when we were given the crushing, debilitating, life-changing news about Stephanie. I refused to relive it. I would grieve in my own way and they could grieve in theirs.

I would cry alone.

Early Monday morning, we met with the doctor and signed the necessary papers. They would start whole brain radiation today.

4/13—Started with low dose of radiation—will work up to regular dosage. Dermatologist took sample of blisters—check to see what is going on—Dr. Turner and Theresa stopped in—don't worry about staying in hospital—will get her back into oncology dept. Didn't know I should be worrying about that now—too many other things to worry about—awake often, then dozing—appeared to have a few mini seizures—staring, eyes wide open, breathing heavy, drawing arms up and then relaxing.

4/14—Radiation treatment at 10:30—IV put in for antibiotic—Doctors say Steph's opening of eyes very wide, breathing heavy and small movement of arms might indicate pressure on brain stem from swelling—No! No! No! When will things get better? Ever?

The days, the radiation treatments, the journal entries continued, without much change. Stephanie tenaciously fought all of the problems that had plagued her for many weeks. Slowly, we were settling into another fairly predictable pattern. And the days dragged on.

April nineteenth. Easter Sunday. I had considered preparing an Easter basket for Stephanie, but the thought of seeing her lying there, not able to hunt for the basket or eat the candy, gave me a sad, sinking feeling. If this was going to be her last Easter, I didn't want to remember the holiday as it would be today.

I wanted to remember her excitement and enthusiasm as she, still in her pajamas, hair tousled, eyes still bleary with sleep, combed the whole house hunting for her treasure of jelly beans, chocolate rabbits, yellow chicks, foil-wrapped eggs, and small trinkets all cradled in a nest of green grass in her brown and pink woven basket. I wanted to remember her pulling open drawers, looking into closets, peering behind doors, scrambling up on chairs to look on shelves, and peeking into corners. I wanted to remember her in a fit of excited giggling and prancing when she accidentally found her sisters' baskets. I wanted to remember her look of dismay and impatience, the frustration in her voice when she couldn't find her basket, and she would ask, "Okay, where did the Easter bunny hide my basket? Am I hot or cold?"

I was desperate to remember the way everything used to be, not as it was now.

The next day, Lydia came in to give Stephanie her morning bath. I stood on the other side of the bed, handing her the soap, rinsing the wash cloth in the basin, passing her the lotion, helping to turn Stephanie, and exchanging idle chatter.

"I'll brush her hair. I like doing that." As I stroked her head with the brush, the hair clung to the bristles. I couldn't believe what I was seeing. Her hair was coming out in large clumps. *No, no, not so soon. Not all at once.*

I looked across the bed at Lydia. She was staring at the bare spots on Stephanie's head. Tears filled her eyes, and she hurried around the bed and crushed me against her bosom.

Youth fades, love droops, the leaves of friendship fall,
A mother's secret hope outlives them all.

Oliver Wendell Holmes

I hadn't left Stephanie for more than an hour at any time since we had entered the hospital, so when Ronnie broached the subject of a dinner with Bob and Barb, friends from our home town, I wasn't exactly enthusiastic.

"They want to take us to dinner Saturday evening." He stood at the bottom of Stephanie's bed, scanning her latest chart, looking for something to do that would keep him from looking at me, not wanting to see the unwillingness on my face. He knew I would struggle with the thought of leaving Stephanie. "They'll take us some place close to the hospital so you don't have to be gone for a long time." He looked at me now, still sitting in my chair by the window. "You know, it's time that you get out of here for a while." I could hear the urgency in his voice. I could sense that he was expecting my response to be negative. "Sitting in this room day after day isn't doing you *or* Stephanie any good." He moved to the window and watched the branches of a nearby tree whip in the wind; the same tree that I watched every day.

How could I explain that I had no desire to leave the hospital, that I had no desire to leave this room, that I had no desire to leave this chair, that I had no desire to leave Stephanie, that I had no desire to become part of the world again, that I was too tired, that I was drained of any emotion, that I just wanted to shrink inside of myself and disappear.

"I can't go out to dinner. I don't have any decent clothes here." I continued staring out the window at the raindrops dripping from the overhang. Plop, plop, plop. The drops falling on the window sash kept the same steady beat as the life-giving machines.

"I'll come down and sit with Stephanie while you drive home, get a real shower, have time to do your nails, or whatever you want to do, get dressed, and come back in time for dinner." Eagerness and apprehension filled his voice as he looked at me, with a small pleading smile spreading over his face, and fidgeted with his car keys.

Still, I sat staring out the window, listening to the rhythm of the raindrops, the faint, familiar hum of the heating unit, and the pacifying, ever—present beat of the machines. This was my world. This was my comfort. This was all I knew. This was all I wanted to know.

"Okay."

Walking across the bridge that connected the hospital to the parking garage, I felt strangely disoriented, disconcerted, and confused. How long had it been since I had walked outside the hospital by myself? How long had it been since I'd ridden in a car? How long had it been since I'd driven a car? How long had it been since I'd been away from Stephanie for any length of time? I knew the answers to all of those questions, and it didn't make me feel any more confident or composed.

The garage was dark and damp, smelling of oil and gas fumes. I clutched the parking ticket and car keys in my sweaty, shaking hand, wondering which way I should go. I spotted our dark blue Ford Crown Victoria as I turned the corner.

My heart began pounding. Can I do this? I wanted to turn and run back into the safety of the hospital. Should I do this? I wanted the security that I felt when sitting beside Stephanie's bed. My inner-voice was screaming at me to go back and sit in the chair that had become my haven, my sanctuary, my home away from home.

Stop it, I admonished myself. You can do it, you should do it, and you need to do it.

I turned the key and heard the familiar hum of the engine. Gripping the steering wheel, I backed out of the parking space, and began inching down the narrow, winding, cement lane to the exit. My hand shook as I handed the money to the smiling garage attendant.

As the exit gate swung up, panic set in. Which way do I turn? Perspiration was running down my sides, my head was throbbing, my legs were shaking, and I was so disoriented that I didn't know what to do next. I sat, transfixed. I couldn't move.

"Ma'am, is there a problem? The gate's open. You can leave."

From a distance, I heard the attendant's words. I sat clutching the steering wheel.

"Ma'am?" He leaned out of the window of his small cubicle. "Are you okay?" Terrified, I eased out of the garage and turned into the oncoming traffic. Horns blared. Brakes screeched. I glanced in my rearview mirror, saw a large truck bearing down on me, yanked the steering wheel to the right, pulled over to the side of the road, and sat with my head in my hands. I could feel my heartbeat pounding in my ears. There was a strange, rushing, roaring, thunderous sound inside of my head. I looked up and tried to focus on the road and the cars passing by. Everything seemed to be floating in slow-motion. I was strangely dizzy and weak. Beads of perspiration trickled down my face.

What's happening to me? Am I having a panic attack? Am I suffering from sleep deprivation? Is it a combination of both? I took deep breaths, relaxed my arms and legs, and tried to clear my mind. I could beat this. I would beat this. Whatever it was. I sat, watching the cars whiz by, trying to get myself under control.

Cautiously, I eased back into the flow of traffic and squinting into the afternoon sun, forced myself to concentrate on the road, determined to get home as quickly as I could. Then I could get back to the hospital where I belonged.

As I drove down our lane, it felt strangely unfamiliar to me. Nothing had changed, but it wasn't Stephanie's hospital room.

I unlocked the back door and stepped into the kitchen. The phone was ringing. "Carole, you need to get back to the hospital right away. Stephanie's been having seizures, big ones, one right after the other, ever since you left."

My head was spinning. The lines of the pattern on the wallpaper began floating up and down. Holding the phone, I sank to the floor.

"The doctors aren't sure what's happening, but they want you here. Right away." Ronnie's voice was shaking.

169

I rushed out the door, tore down the lane, and headed back to the hospital. Oh, God, I prayed, silently, please don't let Stephanie die before I get there. Please. Please. Please. Don't let her suffer.

I sped down the highway, darting and weaving through the traffic. Thoughts of desperation and fear battled with pleas of hope and longing in my head, each vying for control of my mind.

Why, why, why did I leave her when I knew I shouldn't? Did she know I left? Was that why she was having the seizures? Can she *will* herself to hang on till I get there?

Of course you can hang on my Special Angel. You've done it before. You can do it again. I love you Stephanie. Hang on Sweetheart, hang on. The battle continued on inside of my head.

I was tearing down the highway, blowing my horn, cutting in and out of traffic, swerving from lane to lane.

But, this time she probably can't make it. The doctors want me there. They must know she's dying. They said hurry. I love you Stephanie. I'll never leave you again. I should have told Ronnie to tell her that I love her. If she dies, I'll never forgive myself for not being there with her. Silently, the thoughts and pleas continued their struggle for control of my mind.

And then I realized that these weren't silent thoughts any longer. With tears streaming down my face, I was shouting, "I love you, Stephanie. Hang on, Babe, hang on. Mommy's coming." Over and over again, I shouted, *willing* her to hear my words.

I raced down the hallway, punched the elevator button, and watched the lights. Hurry, I begged.

Clambering out of the elevator, I sprinted down the hallway to Stephanie's room. Please, don't let Stephanie be gone. Please.

The door was closed. Why was the door closed? I burst into the room. Her twitching, convulsing body was there, surrounded by doctors and nurses, and thumping, hissing, beeping and pulsing machines.

Ronnie dashed to my side and grabbed me as I felt myself collapsing in relief. She was still alive.

"She's doing better," he said, hastening to assure me. "She's still having seizures, but they've slowed down and they're not as intense."

I broke down and sobbed, all of the pent-up emotions that I had struggled with on my wild ride to the hospital pouring through my body.

Making my way to Stephanie's bedside, I stroked her arm. "Mommy's here, sweetheart," I whispered, leaning over the railing. "Mommy loves you very, very, very much," I said, attempting to remind her of one of the many *love games* we played. I knew she wouldn't respond, but I hoped that she could hear me.

Yes, she was doing better. The thumping, hissing, beeping and pulsing of the machines were the working sounds of life. I hated those machines, but I was thankful for them now.

All evening the seizures persisted. All evening the doctors and nurses worked on Stephanie. All evening we listened to the rhythm of the machines. All evening we stroked, we kissed, we soothed, we talked, and we waited.

Finally, the doctors were confident that Stephanie's seizures were under control, her vital signs were stable, and she was resting peacefully.

I felt my stiff, tense body crumbling in relief. We had weathered one more crisis. Now we would begin again. We would work through the many steps that it would take to get her to the point where she would respond with nods, puckered lips and kisses, pointing fingers, faint smiles, and responses to the therapists' commands.

When the doctors and nurses checked Stephanie's vital signs and machines, for the last time, and left the room, it was approaching midnight. "Do you think we could find something to eat here in the hospital?" Ronnie stood by the window, reflected in the light that shone from the head of Stephanie's bed, his shirt rumpled and sweat-stained.

"I know you don't want to leave Stephanie, but we haven't eaten anything since lunchtime. Maybe we could find a machine with crackers or candy bars." He stretched his legs and flexed his arms, waiting for my response.

Could I break my promise?

As the days wore on and the radiation treatments continued, there were fewer and less intense seizures, but there were also fewer responses to our attempts to get Stephanie to interact with us. Determined not to give up, I continued talking, singing, stroking, massaging, exercising, and cuddling Stephanie. Maybe she couldn't respond, but she could absorb. I would make sure that she knew we were there loving and caring for her. When my body rebelled and wouldn't allow me to stand by the bed and nurture her any longer, I sat in the chair and wrote in my journal.

A constant stream of doctors and nurses came in and out of Stephanie's room checking on the numerous problems that kept cropping up. There was blood in her urine; there was a battle between diarrhea and constipation because of the inability to identify the correct amount of food needed to maintain her weight and nutrition; The nutritionist worried over her ever-changing weight because of the constant adjustments made in the amount of food pumped through her feeding tube; the feeding tube was constantly infected; they continually checked the fluctuating levels of Tegretol and Decadron; the therapists did range of motion exercises, trying desperately to keep her limbs loose and mobile so she would be able to respond physically, should she regain what she had lost since the seizures had returned in earnest; they began fitting and making new braces for her feet and legs, attempting to prevent more contractures; they checked and changed levels of the blood thinner, Coumadin; they checked to find out why her eyes were swelling and matting shut; they took the catheter out hoping to stop the cloudy and bloody urine; they looked for reasons why her breathing was heavy and raspy; they continued to deal with the blisters from the staph infection; they checked out the swelling in her knees; they began fitting and modifying a wheelchair for Stephanie's departure; they talked to us about the possible need to go into a nursing home; and they kept evaluating Stephanie's condition in order to determine what should happen next.

The suggestion of a nursing home kept coming up, and I didn't want to hear those conversations and least of all, I didn't want to participate in them. But, I couldn't avoid talking about Stephanie's future any longer.

The pressure was building from all sides. The insurance company wanted Stephanie out of the hospital, for obvious reasons, and the hospital administrators wanted Stephanie out of the hospital because the doctors could no longer prove to them that there was anything more they could do for her once her radiation treatments were finished. And the doctors themselves wanted Stephanie to leave the hospital because they were feeling the pressure from the hospital administrators.

When Dr. Turner and Theresa came into Stephanie's room, carrying several folders, I noticed that, once again, Dr. Turner was wearing a white coat instead of his familiar Mr. Rogers' sweater. I liked him better in his sweater. Theresa spread a number of pamphlets out on the bedside table, while Dr. Turner busied himself checking out Stephanie.

Theresa, a dark-haired, short, plump young woman wore a perpetual smile, so it was hard to tell when she had bad news or good news.

Oh no, I thought, as I glanced at one of the pamphlets. I recognized the familiar structure of a medical facility. This was about nursing homes.

"You know we've been talking to you recently about the possibility of having to move Stephanie out of the hospital and into a nursing home, and now it seems as though we have to put the process in motion." Now her smile turned sad and apologetic. She was on our side and had fought hard to get the insurance company and the hospital to allow Stephanie to stay as long as she had, so I knew this was a difficult matter for her to address.

"I have several pamphlets with information about two different homes here in the area. One is a chronic care facility, and the other one is . . . well, they cater to children." She glanced at Stephanie, then nervously straightened the already orderly pamphlets. Hurriedly, she added, "Although, they said they do, on occasion, take older patients . . . on an individual basis." She turned her head and stared in Dr. Turner's direction, looking for support. Now I knew why he wasn't in his familiar, comfortable, non-threatening sweater. The closing of the ranks.

I was aware that the one that catered to children had a better reputation than the chronic care facility. Why couldn't Stephanie have access to the best?

"Stephanie operates on the level of a child." My voice was angry and frustrated. Stephanie was a child. Couldn't they see that? Yes, chronologically she was an adult, but she was a child in every other way. I could feel the aggravation of days, weeks, months and years of ineffective and sometimes disastrous dealings with doctors and hospitals building inside me. I glared at Dr. Turner, unleashing all of my anger and frustration in his direction with a silent stare.

"Well, we will try, but age is most always the determining factor." Dr. Turner adjusted his tie, jammed his hands into his white coat pockets, and hurried around the bed to stand beside Theresa. His face flushed pink and his voice was defensive. The unforeseen bitterness in my voice had startled him.

"We'll read the pamphlets, but we're not considering a nursing home in this area." Ronnie glanced at Theresa and then turned and looked at Dr. Turner. Then his eyes rested on Stephanie. "And, quite frankly, we're not seriously considering a nursing home, period." He picked up a pamphlet and began flipping through it, but his eyes were still on Stephanie.

I couldn't deal with anything more right now. But, as hard as I tried to repress thoughts of a nursing home, several questions kept coming back. We didn't want Stephanie in a nursing home, but could we give her the care that she needed? And one question that kept wriggling and squirming its way into my thoughts was more important than any other. Was it fair to Stephanie for us to take her home when the medical care she could get in a nursing home would probably be better than what we could provide?

But, finally, it all came down to what we all knew. She needed to be with us.

I knew that the bulk of Stephanie's care would fall upon me, and I was determined that I would be prepared to take care of her. I would learn everything that I needed to know. I would have to learn how to give her insulin shots in her stomach for her diabetes.

I would practice giving shots into an orange.

But, one thought never left my mind. I would have to do all of these procedures at home without the safety net of the doctors and nurses. I was petrified.

174

Did I want to go home? Yes. But I was terrified that I would make a critical mistake when administering Stephanie's medications, operating her feeding tube, or working her suctioning machine. My stomach churned at the thought of holding Stephanie's survival in my hands.

Though I wasn't a part of what was happening in my family's lives since Stephanie and I had arrived at the hospital on February 19th, I was kept aware of what was going on through their many visits and phone calls.

One day Jennifer bounced into Stephanie's room, still in her uniform, smelling of sweat and leather and covered with dust, having just pitched a softball game at a community college close to the hospital. As she recounted the game, pitch by pitch, inning by inning, excitement filling her voice, she kept glancing at Stephanie. Was she feeling guilty because she was happy about winning a softball game while Stephanie was fighting for her life? Was she remembering how Stephanie attended all of her games, holding George, talking with all of the players and coaches, visiting with the parents of the players, drinking a Dr Pepper, and always cheering her on? Was she imagining playing her games, living her life without Stephanie ever again being a part of it?

Was she remembering that, despite Stephanie's mental and physical disabilities, Stephanie still maintained the position of her older sister with a stern reprimand when Jennifer did anything that she disapproved of? Was she remembering how Stephanie occasionally admonished her, shaking her determined, crooked finger at her while staring up into her face? Was she remembering the times when riding in the car together, she would beat a rhythm on the steering wheel while Stephanie strummed an imaginary guitar, both singing and accompanying a song that was playing full-blast on the radio?

Now, as I watched Jennifer standing at the bottom of the bed, basking in the warmth of her most recent victory, I knew that, somewhere in her heart and mind, she was trying to come to grips with the pending absence of Stephanie in her life.

Robyn and Jim were having a house built and, as often happens, it wasn't going to be ready by the date it had been promised. So, Robyn was asking if they could move in with us in May and stay until the house was finished.

"Of course, you can live with us, you know that." I jumped up from my chair and hugged her. "It'll be wonderful to have you all under one roof for a while." I was feeling an excitement, an anticipation, an eagerness that I hadn't felt in a long time. There would be new life in the house. The girls would be a distraction from the fear that threatened to engulf me when I thought about taking Stephanie home, and Robyn would be a big help.

As I thought about Robyn's relationship with Stephanie, how she was always there for her, looking after her, nurturing her, the same words kept coming into my mind. Words that I had spoken to Robyn so many years ago, after our visit with Dr. Patterson.

Stephanie will have to have someone look after her for all of her life.

Had my words robbed Robyn of her childhood? Did she, at the moment I spoke those words, so many years ago, mentally see Stephanie as her future liability? Did she see herself as her sister's caretaker? Was that why when Stephanie didn't do what I asked, and warned her that if she didn't do whatever it was by the time I counted to five I would punish her, Robyn would frantically grab Stephanie and hurry her to do whatever needed to be done? Was that why, at the age of eleven, she hid a doll dress under her shirt and tried to take it out of the store when Stephanie had begged for it, and I told her she couldn't have it? Was that why she never complained when, as a developing pre-teen, she had little privacy during the years of Stephanie's program through the Institutes for the Achievement of Human Potential?

We had never talked about the day that I had spoken those words . . . *Stephanie will have to have someone look after her for all of her life.* I wanted to. I should have. I couldn't.

Now . . . there was nothing to talk about.

Since the end of the radiation treatments was nearing, the doctors ordered an MRI to determine if there had been any change in the tumor.

We were ecstatic. The test showed that the original tumor and the part that extended into the right temporal lobe had actually gotten smaller which, they explained, was highly unusual this early in treatment. We couldn't contain the warm glow that spread through our bodies and extended across our faces in wide smiles.

But, then, our happiness was tempered with anxiety when they pointed out that the diffused area of the tumor looked the same. It hadn't shrunk. However, they said, we shouldn't allow that to upset us, because it didn't really mean anything, since it was possible that instead of the tumor, what they were seeing *could* be scar tissue caused by the radiation.

We would cling to that thought, that possibility, that hope.

I began practicing giving Stephanie her shots, measuring and pouring the medications into her tubes, filling and monitoring the tube that held her liquid food, and applying the medication to the site of her feeding tube. I felt quite capable under the watchful eyes of the nurses.

Suddenly, after all this time, 3 months and 8 days, we were going home, Wednesday, May twenty-seventh, two days after Memorial Day. Except for nagging little problems with minor infections, excess fluid, and fluctuating weight, the doctors were pleased with Stephanie's over-all stability. Her seizures were now nothing more than slight tremors, which occurred on rare occasions.

This was *the* day. This was what we had waited for. What we had longed for. And now that *the* day was here, my emotions were totally out of control. They raged from euphoria, jubilation, and unreserved elation, to powerful waves of anxiety, apprehension, and trepidation. I felt powerless to move beyond the hospital. I retreated to my chair.

My sanctuary.

Everything was ready at home. The supplies had been delivered, the insurance company had okayed home healthcare personnel, and Robyn and her family had moved in. No more reasons. No more excuses.

I had asked Ronnie to go to the bakery and get a large sheet cake for all of the staff on the eighth floor to enjoy.

Throughout the morning, nurses, doctors, aides, technicians and therapists all came into the room to say good-bye. They hugged Stephanie's non-responsive body, told her they were pulling for her, they would miss her, and they loved her. Then they would embrace me, tell me they wished us all well, they knew we would take good care of Stephanie, and they'd never forget her or the love that surrounded her.

With each embrace and kind word, I could feel the protective shield, the poorly constructed facade that I used as a barrier between me and the pain-ridden world begin to weaken. And when everyone else was gone and Lydia approached me, I felt the barrier I had so ineptly built being washed away in a torrent of tears.

Lydia and I stood in the middle of the room, arms entwined around each other's back. "I know you'll take good care of Stephanie." She wiped at the tears running down her face with the back of her hand. Then, loosening her arm from our embrace, she grasped my elbow and led me to the side of Stephanie's bed. "I want you to know that I'll say a prayer for Stephanie every day." Her free hand stroked Stephanie's face. "I won't bother you by asking you to keep in touch with us because I know how busy you'll be. But, I'll know what's happening because I'll keep in touch with Dr. Turner." She released my elbow and grasped both of my hands. "I want you to know that I am honored to have had the opportunity to take care of Stephanie, and I'm extremely happy that I had the chance to get to know you." Her chin quivered and her sad, brown eyes caressed my face. "I know you don't see it, think it, or feel it, but you're a very special person."

My tears stained her crisp, mustard-colored uniform as she held me for one last time.

When everyone had left the room, all of our belongings had been packed and taken to the first floor, and we were waiting for the ambulance and the escort, I realized that Dr. Turner hadn't been among the well-wishers. I was disappointed. Yes, I had aimed some anger and frustration in his direction on occasion, at times by glaring at him and at times by ignoring him, but he had been special to Stephanie from the first day when he had told her she could call him Bill, and he had been our stanch, steadfast, stalwart, ally and fount of information from the very beginning. I needed to say good-bye to him. I needed to thank him. I needed to let him know how much we appreciated the many hours that he spent with Stephanie, with me, not only during normal working hours, but long after his workday should have ended.

And then I heard the faint, familiar squeak of his soft-soled shoes on the waxed floor. When I looked up, he was standing in the doorway, his faded, worn, blue cardigan sweater hanging loosely from his slightly-rounded shoulders. He was holding a yellow folder against his chest.

"I was afraid I might miss you." He smiled, placed the folder on the bedside table, and stood staring down at Stephanie. Not taking his eyes off of Stephanie, he pointed his finger at the folder. "I have information and forms that you'll need."

"So, our girl is ready to travel, is she?" He gathered Stephanie's tiny hand into his long, thin fingers, raised it to his lips, and then gently replaced it on the bed.

Still staring at Stephanie's placid, unseeing, expressionless face, he said, "You know I'll be seeing Stephanie again." Cautiously, he lowered himself and sat on the edge of her bed, rubbing her arm. Was he reassuring me or himself?

I nodded. Would he be seeing her again? We were scheduled to return to the hospital to see him on June tenth, just two weeks from now, but would she still be here to keep the appointment? We had been told that, realistically, she could *possibly* live another six months and, perhaps, at best, a year. But, in the last few months, I had learned that I shouldn't, couldn't, depend on everything that I was told.

"Are you going to be okay?" He lifted his lanky frame from the bed and stood facing me.

Am I going to be okay? I could no more answer that question than I could explain where a cloud goes when it's not in the sky, or where a tear goes when it's not in your eye, or where fire goes when you blow out the flame.

"Yes, I'll be okay." I put an exaggerated smile on my face. "I'm excited about going home, but I'm scared too."

"Of course, you're scared. I'm a little nervous myself."

My heart lurched. Dr. Turner was nervous? No, no, no, I pleaded silently; don't let me know that you're just like the rest of us. Don't allow me to see any weakness in you.

The room seemed to be shrinking. Things were not like I wanted them to be. I didn't want him to admit that he was nervous; I wanted him to reassure me that everything was going to be just fine.

"I'm nervous because I want so badly for everything to go well for all of you." He had sensed the anxiety and disappointment in me and had seen the fear on my face when I heard his confession. "And things will go well for you because Stephanie has been stable for awhile now. Yes, she has some lingering, nagging problems, but none of them are life-threatening." His voice took on a convincing urgency as he tried to blank out the words that had shaken me. He placed his hand on my shoulder. "If you need anything, if you have any questions or concerns, don't hesitate to call me. Day or night."

Tell him now. Let him know that his comfort, his compassion, his judgment, his decision—making, his genuine caring, and the giving of his precious time will always be remembered and appreciated. I stood motionless. Tears filled my eyes. The words went unspoken.

As he turned and walked away, I stood and looked around the room like I was seeing it for the first time. No tape player. No tapes. No George. No hairbrush. No special soap. No special lotion. No foot braces. No wheelchair. Other than Stephanie lying in the bed, there were no signs that she had ever been here. And, in a few minutes, *she* would be gone.

The living room was stacked full of boxes. Bed linens, blue moisture pads, cans of liquid nourishment, sterile applicators, gauze pads, rubber gloves, diapers, mouth care products, peroxide, alcohol, leg and foot splints, insulin and needles, a suction machine, blood pressure equipment, a machine that, when plugged into the wall, would hiss, pulse, beep and thump while dispensing food and medicine, and a wide variety of medications, all surrounded a hospital bed. We were home.

When I had met with the nutritionist, the physical and occupational therapists, the oncologist, and the gastroenterologist, to discuss Stephanie's discharge from the hospital and placement into home care, I had listened to their words, signed their papers, nodded when appropriate, and feigned understanding. Now, alone, and not distracted by the overwhelming technicalities of it all, I sat down and read what I should do, how I should do it, and when I should do it. Our lives would revolve around the schedule I was preparing.

The insurance company had scheduled home healthcare nurses' aides to come three days a week, for two hours a day, the nurse would come once a week, and the physical and occupational therapists would each come for one hour a week. I was thankful that our weekends would be free from intrusion by anyone associated with healthcare.

From the very beginning, I didn't want any of them coming into our house on a regular schedule. If I needed them, I would call them. I knew that wasn't how it worked, but I resented strangers coming into our home trying to do what I wanted, needed, to do for Stephanie. They didn't know her, they didn't know all that she'd been through, they didn't know what she liked, they didn't know what made her feel better, they didn't know how to do what I had been helping to do for her for the past three—and—a—half months.

And they didn't love her.

Alice, a tall, middle-aged woman, with a shy, hesitant smile, looked around the living room, still crowded with boxes of supplies. Her bleached-blonde, permed hair touched the top of the collar on her spotless, starched uniform. Her white shoes were scuffed and stained.

She placed her packet of papers on the table next to the bed, fastened her slender, chafed fingers around the metal bed rail, and looked down at Stephanie with warmth and compassion spreading across her face. She turned slightly to look at me. "So, tell me about Stephanie. Tell me what happened to her." She reached down and stroked her arm.

I stared at her coldly. She wasn't going to win me over by asking questions, showing interest in what Stephanie had been through, and demonstrating concern. She wasn't going to commandeer my responsibilities. She wasn't going to crack my resolve. But, most of all, she wasn't going to steal away time that *I* could spend with Stephanie. Precious time. *My* time.

For several weeks, I kept Alice at arm's length. I allowed her to prepare the water and watch me as I bathed Stephanie. I allowed her to hand me the soap, the washcloth, the towel, the lotion, the mouth care products, the diaper. I allowed her to help carry Stephanie from the bed into the borrowed recliner that lifted, shifted, thrust, and maneuvered to make it easier to move Stephanie from her bed into a sitting position and then get her out of the chair and back into her bed.

I wasn't rude to her, but I made it clear that I didn't need her. I made sure that she understood I was capable of caring for Stephanie. I made it obvious that she was an outsider. She wasn't part of me or mine.

Stephanie's hospital bed sat against the outside, back wall of the living room of our log house, surrounded by the pumping, hissing machine, boxes of hygiene materials stacked on a small, wooden, rectangular table, and a small blue and white plastic stepping stool that made it easier for the grandchildren to climb onto Stephanie's bed.

Yes, Stephanie was still non-responsive, but we encouraged the girls to touch her, talk to her, read to her, sing to her, and reintroduce to her the many favorite keepsakes that she kept in her over-sized pocketbook that her friend Mary Lee had given her. She never carried the pocketbook outside of the house but, instead, used it to store and contain her valuables—a book about Curious George, buttons, necklaces, adjustable rings, playing cards, a bundle of store coupons clipped from the Sunday paper, magic markers, index cards, a small multi-colored troll with purple hair, rubber bands, a small change purse filled with coins, George's pacifier, tissues, a hairbrush, a comb, a wristwatch with no wristband, and notes to and from Carroll Mitchell. She kept her pocketbook, along with other keepsakes, crammed into the toy chest in her bedroom.

Stephanie had always made her bedroom off limits to the girls. She would play with them once in a while, but she liked her solitude and her privacy, so her bedroom became her escape, her inner—sanctum.

And she didn't allow the girls to touch anything in her pocketbook and only on rare occasions would let them hold George, after much begging, while she stood guard watching their every move only to snap him from their arms after just a few seconds. So though being allowed to play with Stephanie's most treasured possessions was enticing, they were still hesitant. She didn't look like the Aunt Stephanie that they knew.

To relieve the girls' anxiety, we tried to explain what had happened to Aunt Stephanie and why she spent most of her time in bed hooked up to a machine, but it was easy to see from the puzzled looks on their little faces that none of what we were saying was making much sense to them. Now that she was home, shouldn't she be better, they wondered?

They were afraid of the tube that projected from her stomach, snaked from beneath the sheet, and climbed to the plastic bags that hung suspended from the pole like balloons filled with colored liquids. They couldn't figure out why her eyes were open, but she wasn't seeing them. They didn't understand why she wasn't answering when we talked to her.

But, after a few days, when they understood that she, and all of her apparatus, wasn't going to hurt them, and they wouldn't hurt her by being in her bed, they looked forward to playing with her.

My bed would be the sleeper-sofa that sat against the inside wall of the living room, facing the fireplace on the opposite wall.

Without expressing our expectations, or setting rules, or assigning duties, we settled into a routine. Robyn took over the household duties and the care of the girls, Jennifer went to her life—guarding job and helped out with whatever needed to be done when she came home, Ronnie taught his summer classes at the college, mowed the lawn, and ran errands, Jim traveled back and forth to his job as a high school guidance counselor, checked on the progress of their house, helped Robyn with the cooking and the girls, and I spent the majority of my time tending to Stephanie.

I made sure that I did my swimming pool duties before Alice arrived because I didn't want to have anything to do that might interfere when it was time to bathe and tend to Stephanie. I was certain that Alice would jump at the chance to take over my duties. Lately, she had been hinting that I should use the time when she was there to do some other things around the house. She even suggested that I might use the time to leave the house and do something for myself. How dare she make such a blatant attempt at getting me out of the house so that *she* could take over *my time* with Stephanie.

I was tired. Very tired. I couldn't ignore it any longer. Waking up every two hours to change and turn Stephanie, and then tending to her all day long was sapping my strength and energy. Yes, when we were in the hospital, I did wake up every two hours to watch, or to help, with Stephanie's care, but I could occasionally rest during the afternoon when Ronnie arrived. I didn't lie down or nap, but I could sit in my chair, close my eyes, allow my mind to wander beyond the hospital walls, away from the stark reality of what was happening every day to Stephanie and how I was powerless to do anything about it, how I was powerless to make it all go away, how I was powerless to change the direction that our lives were taking.

Everyone in the family offered to help take care of Stephanie, but I couldn't shake this need to be in control of her care. I *needed* her to need me. I needed to assuage the guilt that plagued me for not being able to make her whole again. I needed to alleviate the guilt that assailed me daily for not being the one who was terminally ill.

Children weren't supposed to die before their parents.

But the most crippling guilt came from acknowledging that I was pathetically shallow and selfish. As much as I wanted Stephanie to live, I realized that I *couldn't* unequivocally say that I would choose to die in her place. I *thought* I would. I wanted to *think* I would, but I just wasn't one hundred per cent sure I would. What kind of mother was I? Why couldn't I, without reservation, declare that I would, if it were possible, take on the pain and suffering of my children and willingly die in their place?

Selfishly, I reasoned, if I should die in Stephanie's place, yes, she would live, but I would still be without her. I wanted us both to live. I *needed* us both to live.

I wanted it all.

Unlike when I was in the hospital, though it was my own choice, I wasn't getting any rest, day or night; I wasn't getting a brief reprieve from the reality that stared us all in the face each day.

By the end of June, when Steph had been home for a little over a month, I realized, as difficult as it was for me to admit it, I needed Alice's help. Just a little. I began allowing Alice to bathe Stephanie on occasion, while I watched her every move.

But, I ignored her suggestion that while she bathed Stephanie, I might go outside and sit by the pool and relax. She wasn't going to displace me that easily.

I knew in my head that what I was doing was childish, selfish, and plain ridiculous, but my heart wouldn't allow me to relinquish any part of Stephanie to anyone else. As the summer wore on, however, my resolve to defend my territory, maintain my control, and stave off Alice's attempt to appropriate valuable minutes and hours with Stephanie began to diminish, and I relinquished even more of Stephanie's care to her. I discovered that I genuinely liked her. Indeed, she was a kind, loving, caring, capable nurses' aide. She had won me over, despite my stubborn determination to close her from our lives.

I found that I could go outside and work on the pool while Alice bathed Stephanie and the world didn't collapse around us. I discovered that she knew how to do range of motion exercises with deft precision and expertise, and I observed her putting the braces on Stephanie's feet and legs, all the while talking to her in a loving and nurturing tone, just as I always did. Maybe, I decided, she did love Stephanie. And it was okay with me.

When we took Stephanie back to the hospital for her first visit, the doctors didn't find anything to indicate that she was any better or any worse. And when Dr. Turner continued to call, about every ten days, we had nothing to report that would warrant revisiting the hospital. He sounded disappointed, but not surprised, when we gave him the same lackluster account of Stephanie's condition. And, he always asked how we were holding up physically and emotionally, how we were dealing with the overwhelming responsibilities, and did we need more help than we were receiving now? He was his same caring, compassionate, comforting self.

By the middle of July, the school had to know if I was planning to return to the classroom. I had used up all my sick leave, and then I had taken a leave of absence through June. Now I had to make a decision.

I couldn't help remembering what had happened the last time I had left Stephanie for any length of time. What would I do if anything happened to her while I was at school? Could I live with myself if she died when I wasn't with her? Could I carry even one more ounce of guilt than that with which I had already burdened myself?

In Ronnie's mind, the decision wasn't that difficult. Now that I was accepting and trusting Alice, and the insurance company was going to pay for nurses' aides five days a week for four hours a day, and his schedule at the college was so flexible, we could easily cover the whole day while I was gone. I could administer her medications before and after the school day, and, as always I could run her feedings throughout the night. Why was I struggling so with this decision, he wondered, when everything had been worked out? He wasn't unfeeling and unaware of how difficult it would be for me to be away from Stephanie, but he felt I needed to get out and have some semblance of a life beyond the four walls of our house.

He was right. Stephanie's vital signs were stable. There were no indications that the tumor was active again. She hadn't had a seizure since the radiation treatments had ended. And we needed the money.

The insurance company wasn't paying for *all* of the medical supplies, and even fewer of the daily personal care products; the special soaps, lotions, creams, mouth-care needs and diapers. We had accrued bills from her long hospital stay. And more bills were piling up.

I would go back to work.

Sitting at the dining room table with a variety of English books open and spread around my plan book, I still questioned my decision to go back into the school. How would I function in front of a classroom filled with restless students?

The phone rang. I seldom answered it. It was always a concerned, caring, loving, relative or friend, all with good intentions, but there were days when I just couldn't handle talking about Stephanie's condition and our well-being. Whoever answered the phone would identify the caller, look at me for a yes or no response, and then make the appropriate excuses if I chose not to speak to the caller.

"It's Sonny, Carole." Ronnie held the phone in my direction. He didn't wait for a response. Sonny was my principal. Of course, I would talk to him.

Ten minutes later, I hung up the phone, closed my English books, piled them on top of my plan book, stuffed them into my briefcase and collapsed into the chair, smiling broadly.

"What's going on?" Ronnie's tone was wary.

"I'm not going back into the classroom. Sonny wants me to take over in guidance for a counselor who has to be out for the first semester." I couldn't stop smiling. No lesson plans. No papers to grade. An enormous weight had just been lifted from my shoulders, and I knew Sonny had done this to help me out, not because I was the best choice to take the place of the guidance counselor.

Our new homecare schedule started in the middle of August. Another nurses' aide, Ida, was assigned to share the five—day week of duties with Alice. They already knew and liked each other, and because I had finally opened my heart to Alice, it was easy to accept and love the short, blonde, effervescent, witty addition to our household. Ida would help make our lives easier, and it was obvious that she was smitten with Stephanie from the beginning.

She gently stroked Stephanie's arm, and spoke in a soft, tender voice. "Hi, Punkin'," she said. "This is Ida, 'n' I'm gonna take care of you. Real good care of you." Her voice trembled. "You can hear me. I know you can." She leaned down and kissed Stephanie's cheek. "Sweetie Pie, you just hang in there. Ole Ida's here for whatever you need." She cleared her throat and busied herself straightening the bed sheets.

When I had finally welcomed Alice into my home and heart, she had graciously added washing Stephanie's clothes and bed linens to her duties, and when Ida arrived, they began washing all of our clothes. The house was finished, so Robyn and her family were leaving and Jennifer was going off to college; Alice and Ida were doing all in their power to relieve us of extra responsibilities.

How, I wondered, could I have wasted so much time getting to know and appreciate Alice's kind and loving nature? And now, I had two caring, kind, and compassionate nurses' aides to love and appreciate.

Robyn, Jim and the girls moved out on Friday of the Labor Day weekend. I would miss them, but I knew they were anxious to get into their new home and back to their routine. The girls had been good for Stephanie. Even though she didn't respond, somehow I knew she was hearing them, enjoying them, loving them.

Jennifer would be leaving for school on Monday, and her classes would start on Tuesday. I was worried that her thoughts would be at home with Stephanie, and her mind wouldn't be on her studies, but, if things got too bad, she was just ten minutes from Robyn and only an hour away from home. We would do our best to keep her spirits bolstered and her mind free of worry.

On Saturday afternoon, while I was bathing Stephanie, I told her a story about a monkey named Curious George. I told the story often, hoping that hearing George's name might prompt some response.

I worked from the top of her head to the bottom of her feet, all the time telling my story. I rinsed the soap from the washcloth in the pink plastic basin and swabbed between her toes. "And then George . . ."

"Stop!"

I jerked my head up and looked around the room. No one there. Could Ronnie have come back into the house and I didn't hear him? Could Jennifer have called down from her bedroom? "Jennifer," I yelled, "did you call me?"

"No," she shouted down the stairs.

With a queasy, unsettled feeling in my stomach, I returned to swabbing between Stephanie's toes.

"Stop! I said stop!"

My heart lurched. My skin was covered with goose bumps. With my heart in my throat, my pulse throbbing in my ears, I looked up at Stephanie. "Oh, my God. My God." She was looking at me. She was seeing me.

"Stop. You stop." She lifted her weak, shaking arm, just slightly off of the bed, and pointed her skinny, crooked finger at me.

"Ronnie, Jennifer!" I screamed. "She's talking to me!! I dashed to the bottom of the stairs. "Jennifer! Jennifer! Stephanie's talking to me!! Jennifer!!"

I ran out the back door and into the yard shouting, "Ronnie! Ronnie! She's talking!! She told me to stop!" I didn't see him, so I hurried back into the house.

I raced into the living room. Jennifer was standing and staring at Stephanie, a look of disbelief blanketing her face. Stephanie's eyes were moving, looking at Jennifer, surveying everything around her.

Ronnie came running into the room. "What happened?" His face was flushed with fright.

"Stephanie's talking! She told me to stop! She pointed her finger at me!" In a frenzy, I ran around the room, shouting, laughing, and crying. I hugged Ronnie. I hugged Jennifer.

I hurried back to Stephanie. I leaned over the metal bar and kissed her bald head. I wanted to grab her out of the bed and twirl her around the room and sing *You are my sunshine* like I had done so many times before. Instead, I climbed into her bed and held her close.

"Oh, my Special Angel, I love you so much," I repeated over and over again as I pressed her against my heart, tears coursing down my cheeks.

Since Ronnie and Jennifer hadn't heard Stephanie talk, they were a little skeptical. Yes, she was looking around the room, she was following us with her eyes, but had she really spoken?

I would prove it to them. I held her foot and moved the washcloth between her toes.

"Stop! You stop it." A look of irritation, that we knew so well, darkened her face. Her leg jerked as she attempted to pull her foot from my hand.

We looked at each other, beaming.

I couldn't wait to spread the good news to the family, but because it was a holiday weekend, I waited until Tuesday to call Dr. Turner.

"That's great news." His voice was tinged with skepticism. What else could I expect? He was a man of science. He would need to see and hear for himself. We were to bring her to the hospital for an MRI on October first. In the meantime we would document every word, every movement, every response to commands, every sign of improvement.

9/5/92—Saturday—"Stop!" . . . Stop!" . . . ."I said stop!" . . . ."Stop, you stop it!" Pointed finger at me (all of this because I was touching her feet) Looked right at me when Ronnie asked where Mommy was (What a moment! What a thrill!) Used left hand to wipe her nose (Good sign, since she's left-handed)

9/6/92—Sunday—"Stop. Stop. I told you stop" . . . ."Stop I said" . . . ."You stop it" (Again, because I was bathing her. Never imagined that I'd ever be so thrilled to hear the word STOP)

9/7/92—Monday—"Stop it! Stop it! Stop it! Stop it" (Bless her heart. Apparently all of the frustration that she has felt over the last 8 months is pouring out of her) "Stop it, will you please." (She hasn't forgotten her manners) "I want George" (She's truly back . . . she's asking for George) Using left hand more and more

9/8/92—Tuesday—Said "I love you" four times, twice pointing at me (I can't hear it often enough. Never thought I'd ever hear it again) Alice's first day back since Friday . . . . Steph not talking then . . . Told Alice—"Stop it, Alice" (How did she know her name? When she was non-responsive, she had to be hearing everything we said . . . WOW! Unbelievably scary—but wonderful)

9/10/92—Wednesday—Pointed and let Alice know she was "dirty" (Great! We can get a potty chair and eliminate a lot of dirty diapers) Sitting in recliner, pointed and said "bed" . . . tired of sitting in chair (Fantastic—capable of letting her needs be known)

As the days went by, our joy grew by leaps and bounds. Her words weren't always clear, her sentences weren't always complete, her voice was soft and hesitant, her anger and frustration were clearly obvious, but she was doing and saying things that we thought would never happen again.

Now that Stephanie was responsive and showing such great strides in her recovery, it was even harder to go back to school than I had anticipated. I felt like the mother of a burgeoning toddler. I wanted to be a part of every step in her new beginning. I wanted to hear each new word, see each new gesture, follow each new movement, memorize each new facial expression, be the object of every uttered *I love you.*

I was driving everyone at home crazy, but I just had to know what was happening. I phoned Alice, Ida, and Ronnie every chance I had, pumping them for information, peppering them with instructions, and swamping them with reminders. Now that Stephanie was in a state of recovery, I wanted to make sure that they were doing everything that they were supposed to be doing, when they were supposed to be doing it. And being in an office instead of a classroom, I had many opportunities to call and check.

Alice and Ida left detailed notes, cataloging the daily happenings, which I read voraciously, looking for indications that Stephanie was still progressing, petrified that the recovery would slow down or stop all together, or worse yet, she would show signs of regression.

My fears were unfounded. Each day her vocabulary expanded, allowing her to make her wishes known, emphatically. Her arm and leg movements were stronger and more controlled, making it easier for her to pull away from us when she didn't want to be bothered. And her happy, witty personality emerged, though her interactions were still riddled with negative phrases, making sure that we understood how much she hated being poked, prodded, turned, made to wear her braces, and, most of all, doing her range of motion exercises. *Stop* and *don't* were her new favorite words.

At night, lying on the lumpy sofa-bed, with the springs poking into my back, staring at the beamed ceiling, I reveled in the dramatic, unexpected improvement in Stephanie's condition. I was determined to make everything that we had experienced in the hospital a distant, fading memory. All the stress and worry that we had endured was worth it, considering that we had our little girl back. And now that we had something to look forward to each day, excitement and anticipation would replace the pain and fear that had dug deep, gaping wounds in our hearts.

For the first time, I wasn't dreading taking Stephanie to the hospital. I was looking forward to the MRI results. They had to be good. They had to reflect the improvements that had been taking place in Stephanie for the last month. I refused to have a negative thought as we dressed Stephanie and prepared her for her ambulance ride.

I propped her up with pillows and pulled her favorite Mickey Mouse sweatshirt over her head while Ronnie worked on getting sweatpants over her diaper. She had gained so much weight that nothing she owned fit her properly. Leaning over the bed, we tugged and pulled, trying to make the shirt meet up with the pants.

"Daddy, stop!" She delivered a left-handed uppercut to Ronnie's jaw.

His head snapped back, his eyes widened, and his mouth dropped open.

Startled, he looked at me. Equally startled, I looked at him. We burst into laughter and chalked up another memory.

Dr. Turner was just as surprised and thrilled as we had been. He asked her to look up, down, from one side of the room to the other. She did. He asked her if she remembered him and she nodded. He beamed. He asked her to repeat several words for him, but she sat staring straight ahead. He looked at me. I asked her to please say the words and she did. Again, he beamed.

Now we sat in his office waiting for the results of the MRI. This time I felt no need to count tiles or wonder about the pictures on the wall

I heard the soft squeak of his shoes. I looked towards the door just as he bounced into the room, his face glowing, his eyes sparkling.

"The MRI shows that the tumor has shrunk to less than a third of its original size." I couldn't tell if he was breathless from the walk down the hallway or from the excitement of imparting the good news. He couldn't stop smiling.

"Shrinkage of this magnitude, this long after radiation treatments have ended, is almost unheard of." He crossed his arms over his chest like he was trying to keep himself from bursting with delight and disbelief.

I smiled back. I reached over to the wheelchair and held Stephanie's hand. I kept smiling. I felt strangely tranquil and composed. And then I broke down and sobbed with joy.

By the middle of November Stephanie was staying awake for longer periods of time, moving her arms and legs more frequently and beginning to make more sense when she tried to carry on a conversation. Up until now, except for a few phrases that were admonitions and requests, most of her words and phrases seldom connected with anything that was happening at the moment.

Now it was obvious that she was *somewhat* aware of what was going on around her and her comments mostly pertained to the situation. One morning, as I turned off her feeding tube, changed her diaper, and prepared to leave for work, I leaned over the side of the bed, kissed her cheek, rubbed the sparse fuzz that formed a mottled pattern across her head, and caressed her face. "I love you, my Special Angel," I said.

When I straightened up and turned to leave, she touched my hand. "Mommy, don't go." Tears welled in her eyes. "Stay home with me."

Her words hit me in the face like a bucket of cold water.

I clutched the metal rail of the bed and steadied myself. My legs were shaking. "Oh . . . sweetheart, I don't . . . want to leave you . . ." I bit my lip, suppressing the tears that were swelling up inside of me. How could I leave her now?

I slid the bed rail down, climbed in, held her close and rocked her back and forth. She did know what was going on. She was aware when I left her. She was experiencing more emotions than just anger and frustration. She understood much more than I had thought.

What should I do now? More than anything, I wanted to stay with her, but there were so many other things to consider. None more important than Stephanie, certainly, but important nonetheless.

I pulled her closer.

"Stephie, Mommy has to go to work now. She'll be back this afternoon." Ronnie was standing in the doorway. He motioned for me to get out of the bed.

"Daddy will take care of you this morning and then Alice will be here later." He moved to the side of the bed and held her hand and kissed her on her forehead. "How about I put you in the wheelchair and we sit at the table and color?" He waved his hand, signaling for me to leave.

"We'll talk when you get home."

Concentrating on my job was never easy but that day was even more difficult. Did she cry after I left? Did she think I wasn't coming back? Did she think I didn't love her anymore?

How important was money? How important was it that Sonny had gone out of his way to arrange for me to be out of the classroom and in a job that would be less stressful? How important was it that I would have to take a second leave of absence and wouldn't be assured that I would have a job when I was ready to come back?

All very important, but important enough to disregard Stephanie's plea?

That afternoon, when I walked into the living room, Stephanie was sitting in front of the fireplace in her wheelchair brushing the purple hair of the troll that she kept in her pocketbook, while George watched from his perch on the tray of her chair. She looked up and smiled and then returned to her troll. Happy to see me? Couldn't tell. Too occupied.

I kissed her cheek and hurried out to the kitchen where Ronnie was waiting to talk to me.

"You'll be happy to hear that the minute you were out the door the tears stopped and we spent the morning at the kitchen table coloring." He snapped the pop-top on his soda, took a sip, and leaned back in his chair. "And, Alice said she was fine. She didn't ask for you once." His smile said: *see I knew it would be okay*. "You can read everything that Alice said in her note, but, really, it was fine."

So, there hadn't been any tears or questions. *Was* I happy to hear that? Evidently, she had forgotten about me soon after I left. She had had a good day. I breathed a sigh of relief, but, I had to admit, I *was* a little disappointed. I needed her *more* than she needed me.

Everybody would be home for Thanksgiving, arriving the night before so that they could help with the cooking the next morning. The excitement built inside of me. In February I had never imagined that we'd all be together for another Thanksgiving. I knew I'd savor this one more than all the others.

We'd bought some time.

We would make the most of it.

On Thanksgiving morning Stephanie sat at the table in her wheelchair watching as we ate our pancakes, eggs, bacon, sausage, and sweet rolls. Her head turned from one of us to the other as we talked and laughed. She smiled and answered when we spoke to her, but she seemed much more interested in our food. I wished that she could be eating with us, but when the doctors had seen her in October, they expressed fear about her ability to swallow. They warned us not to feed her any solid food.

Now, from the corner of my eye I saw her hand extend towards Ronnie's plate and then snatch a piece of sweet roll and stuff it in her mouth.

"No, Stephanie, no!" I jumped up from my chair, grabbed her chin, and forced her mouth open, fishing the roll out with my fingers.

Stephanie's face crumpled with tears streaking down her cheeks.

"I'm sorry sweetheart." I held her close and rubbed her back.

By afternoon, smells of turkey and stuffing wafting through the air mingled with the sounds of our chatter and laughter as we hustled around the kitchen. It felt so good to laugh. This truly was a time for thanksgiving.

Secretly, I had hoped that Stephanie would tire and want to take a nap during dinner, but she was wide awake, sitting next to me in her wheelchair. I felt guilty with every bite that I took.

A few weeks later, after learning of Stephanie's attempt to eat from Ronnie's plate, Dr. Turner ordered the nutritionist to administer a swallowing test.

As they began the test, I sat next to her, said a silent prayer, and encouraged her to cooperate.

Stephanie would be enjoying a Christmas dinner with us.

Jennifer was home from college, and Robyn, Jim, and the girls would arrive on Christmas Eve as they did every year. We would all get up in the same house on Christmas morning. It was one of our traditions.

Shopping had been a challenge this year, but with Robyn and Jennifer's help, catalog orders, and an occasional rushed trip to the mall, all the gifts were purchased, wrapped and placed under the tree.

I hung the filled stockings from the mantle, checked to see if there was film in the camera, put a Christmas tape in the tape player, made sure that Ronnie had brought in wood for the fire, and collapsed on the couch. Everything was ready for Christmas morning.

Thoughts of this being the last Christmas together crept into my mind, as I watched Stephanie asleep, curled into a ball on her side; George was cradled in her arms, her thin, wispy hair feathered across her pillow.

Everybody knew that they weren't allowed to come downstairs until Ronnie had lit the fire, I had turned on the music, the tree lights had been turned on, and the camera was ready to snap the first picture of Christmas morning, which was always taken on the landing of the stairway with everybody in their pajamas, their hair tousled, and their eyes still heavy with sleep. This year everybody would have to come to the bottom of the stairs and surround Stephanie sitting in her wheelchair. She sat grinning, clutching George, a few stray strands of hair sticking out from under her Santa Claus hat.

As everybody grabbed their stockings, I carried Stephanie's to her and placed it on the tray attached to her wheelchair. I didn't know what to expect. Would she know what to do with it?

Her eyes lit up, she smiled, and worked to grasp the small gift—wrapped packages inside of her stocking. When she had them all out and spread across her tray, she tugged and pulled at the tape to free the wrapping paper. I allowed her to struggle for a few moments and then I loosened a corner of each package. She ripped the paper off of the box of crayons, the latest Kenny Rogers tape, the box of assorted chocolates, the can of Play Dough, and the package of plastic food items.

She shoved her stocking and its contents to the side of the tray and motioned toward the tree. She wanted the big items now.

She tore the wrapping paper from gifts that, like the ones in her stocking, were mostly geared towards re-awakening her memory and improving her motor skills. Of course there were outfits for George and a few outfits that would fit her shrinking body. She was losing weight and starting to look more like our Stephie.

She held each gift up in front of her, waiting for us to ooh and aah. She liked all of her new toys, but George never left her side. Nothing was going to replace George—ever.

And just when I thought it couldn't get any better, she started to sing along with the Christmas music. She knew the tune and the words to Jingle Bells.

Each day, each week, each month that passed was filled with improvements and accomplishments. By the end of February, she was carrying on complete conversations, putting together ten piece wooden puzzles, fitting the correct objects into shapes of circles, squares, rectangles, and triangles, holding her own drinking cup, and singing along with her tapes.

By June her ability to control the trunk of her body had improved so much that the orthopedic clinic built a new wheelchair that would allow for more movement and flexibility.

Stephanie was taking part in all of our activities now. Ronnie had built a ramp from the front porch to the sidewalk so it was easier to get her outside and into the van, for which we had traded in our Ford.

We had become so accustomed to adjusting to Stephanie's handicaps that we no longer thought of our lifestyle as being out of the ordinary.

We took her shopping, George could always use more clothes, and out to eat, for pizza at Pappy's, of course, but she tired easily, so our excursions were few, spaced out and brief. And if family and friends wanted to see her, they came to the house. Stephanie didn't like to be far from the comfort of her chair and her bed.

Because life had begun to seem more normal again, I was able to think about other things besides Stephanie. I began dreaming again about the sunroom I'd always wanted to replace the garage that blocked our view of the pool, and finally—we did it.

Encased with windows on three sides, we filled the room with wicker furniture and a long oak table and chairs that we would use for big dinners on special occasions. The spacious stone patio, at the back of the sunroom, butted up against the garage, which had been lifted by a huge crane and moved to the side, and was enclosed on the other two sides with a short wall, and a fish pond with a waterfall. To make it more private and tie it all together we installed a wooden fence around the patio and the pool.

Now, in late July, I stood looking at the Black-eyed Susans, the Lilies, the Pampas grasses, the Russian Sage, and a variety of shrubs that wound around the meandering stepping stones from the patio to the pool and around the base of the fence, giving the whole area the feel of a vacation resort.

A plan started to formulate in my mind. We should have a Luau. We should celebrate with family and friends. We should show them that Stephanie was doing well and so were we.

While some family and friends visited occasionally, most called and sent cards and flowers. They were hesitant to visit, they said, for fear that they would disturb Stephanie or our schedule. Actually, I knew they felt uncomfortable, not knowing what to say when they would see her. Everyone was aware that she looked quite different now with the weight gain and the semi-bald head because her hair had never fully grown back.

And what do you say to the family of a terminally ill child?

The night of the Luau, as people arrived wearing grass skirts, sarongs, muumuus, floral shirts, and flowers in their hair, we greeted them by draping a Lei around their necks and handing them a card with their given name on one side and the Hawaiian version on the other side.

As they mingled in front of the gaily decorated tables that lined the walls of the patio, sipping Pina Coladas, snacking on macadamia nuts, pineapple chunks, Hawaiian-style chicken, pork and ham, and a variety of rice dishes, they shared their name cards, struggling to pronounce the Hawaiian version, and finding out the names of others.

Stephanie, *Kekepania* in Hawaiian, sat in her wheelchair, dressed in a flashy, multi-colored Hawaiian shirt and shorts, a Lei around her neck and wearing a hot pink, floppy hat, one of many that family and friends had given her to cover her semi-bald head. With George safely tucked in the crook of her arm, she watched, fascinated by the streams of smoke from the Tiki lamps drifting into the night sky, the strings of multi-colored paper lanterns flickering, and the beat of the drums as some people attempted the Hula while others bent over backwards doing the Limbo Dance.

I watched her carefully, not sure how she would respond to so much sensory stimulation. It had been a while since she had been a part of such a large crowd. I needn't worry. She was smiling and swaying to the music.

For the next several months Stephanie continued to improve, so as the holidays neared, I found that I wasn't thinking about them being *the last* ones. I approached every day as though the next day would be a certainty. I wasn't focused on death, but on life and how we could make the most of it. We had no time to waste, but we did have time.

Christmas morning I looked around the room. Robyn was trying to make some semblance of order out of the aftermath by stacking boxes around the tree; Jim was lost in the latest Tom Clancy book; Jennifer was playing dolls with three-year-old Abby; Ronnie, sitting on the floor, was playing a game with Elizabeth and Sarah; and Stephanie was dressing George in his latest outfit. The fire blazed, the lights on the tree, standing in front of the window, cast a multitude of colors that reflected off of the glass, the floor was cluttered with discarded paper and ribbons, the din of conversation was competing with the Christmas music, and the smell of the turkey roasting in the oven permeated the air.

It felt so good not to be wallowing in doubts and insecurity about the future. I sincerely believed that there would be a *next year* with Stephanie.

In January of 1994, my high school faculty and staff decided to have an after-Christmas party at a nearby seafood restaurant, and they were all urging me to attend. I thanked them for wanting me to come, but I told them I couldn't leave Stephanie anymore than I already did each day. However, when Ronnie heard that there was a party, he insisted that we go, if only for a short time. He reminded me that Stephanie was doing well and Jennifer, still on semester break, would be home to look after her. I had to admit that it would be nice to go out some place other than to the hospital, shopping, or eating at Pappy's.

It had been a long hard winter already, with major ice storms, so maybe this would be a welcome break. We would ride with our friends and neighbors, Joe and Amy. Joe, also an English teacher, and I rode to school together.

I started the night out tentatively, feeling guilty for leaving Stephanie for an evening of dining and socializing. Then, as I began interacting, laughing, and sharing small-talk with my co-workers and their spouses, I realized how much I had missed having contact with people who talked about things other than tube-feedings, operations, radiation treatments, medicines, wheelchairs, range of motion exercises, and . . . . *tumors*.

But, when there was a lull in the conversation, my thoughts went back to Stephanie. Was she still awake? Did Jennifer get her out of her chair and put her back to bed? If something went wrong while I was gone, would Jennifer panic? Did Stephanie miss me?

On the way home we talked about the delicious seafood, the good conversation, and the chance to laugh and forget, if only for a little while.

Our walkway, which had been covered with ice for several days, had melted during the afternoon, but now it was frozen over again. As I stepped onto the walkway my feet flew out from under me, and I slammed down on my right side. Excruciating pain shot through my body and I gasped for air.

The emergency room doctor read the x-rays, told me I had three broken ribs, wrapped an elastic brace around my midriff, gave me a shot of morphine, a bottle of morphine tablets, and told me to go home, rest, and not do any lifting.

No lifting? I lifted Stephanie from her bed to her recliner, to her wheelchair, and back to her bed at least five times a day. Ronnie wasn't always around to help. He had evening classes at the college.

Not to worry, Ronnie said. Alice and Ida would continue lifting her during the day, and he would do the lifting when he was home, and when he had to leave, he would put Stephanie where she needed to be before he left.

I didn't object or argue. I was too tired and in too much pain. I had had an allergic reaction to the morphine and was throwing up things that I didn't know I had inside of me. I discovered that it was a painful state of affairs, throwing up, when you had three broken rib. I threw the morphine tablets away.

While I stayed home from school for a week and got to spend more time with Stephanie, she didn't get to spend as much time in her wheelchair or recliner as she liked; although, in the evenings, she was satisfied if I sat by her bed and read her a book. But what she missed most was sitting on my lap on the couch cuddling and playing love games. I couldn't find a substitute for that.

The doctor had said no lifting for six weeks. Six weeks seemed like a lifetime, but we were slowly making it to the end. I was counting the days.

"Mrs. Black, you have a phone call that you should take. It's not an emergency, but it is important." The voice on the intercom startled me as I sat at my desk grading papers. With my heart in my throat, I rushed to the faculty room and grabbed the phone. I was sure it was about Stephanie.

But this time it was about Ronnie. The metal mail boxes at the college had fallen over and landed on his ankle. He was at the hospital, with tendon and ligament damage, but he would be okay. An audible sigh of relief escaped from my mouth. Stephanie was okay.

The phone call made me uneasy. It had always been in the back of my mind, but now it was right out there in front of me. What *would* I do if I got *the call* when I was in school? Yes, she was doing well, but things could change quickly. They wouldn't phone me though, I reasoned. They would send somebody to talk to me.

While that thought calmed me, temporarily, I felt a rush of guilt when I realized that I had been relieved that it was Ronnie in pain and not bad news about Stephanie. But, then, I rationalized my feelings by telling myself that Ronnie and the girls *understood* that Stephanie took priority over everything.

My *no lifting* days were over. I had to trade places with Ronnie. We had managed to stagger our injuries almost within the six week period.

Ronnie sat on the couch with his swollen ankle and foot, dappled in shades of purple, blue, and red, propped up on a stool with an icepack resting on top. I couldn't help smiling. Ice had led to my injury and ice was helping to heal Ronnie's.

Unable are the Loved to die
For Love is Immortality.

Emily Dickinson

We made it through the rest of the winter and into the spring without any more injuries and, despite our inability to move Stephanie around as much as we had before our accidents, we continued with stretching, flexing, twisting, turning, and range of motion exercises. We also introduced a walker into Stephanie's regimen.

We sat Stephanie on the edge of her recliner, positioned the walker in front of her, placed her hands on the metal frame, raised her to a standing position and removed our hands. In the beginning, she simply collapsed back into the recliner seat, but gradually she wavered, wobbled, swayed from side to side, and then hung on for a fraction of a second, her arms shaking and the muscles in her neck tensing as she strained to hold herself in a standing position. Steadily, her stability and strength became apparent. She couldn't sustain the standing for more than three or four seconds, and couldn't take any steps, but she was standing without help from us.

And, although it was only early April, we were already excited to go back to the orthopedic clinic in August and show the doctors what Stephanie had accomplished.

Unfortunately, by August, we didn't have much to show the doctors and the therapists. Sometime in May, we noticed that Stephanie wasn't able to maintain her stance with the walker quite as long as she had before. Her strength was less in June, and still less in July, and by August we couldn't get her to stand at all.

We also noticed that she wasn't able to sit alone as well as she had before. She tended to lean to her left side and lose her balance. I pulled the pillows out of the closet. I would stuff them around her when she was in the wheelchair and the recliner.

I remembered how I had used pillows when Stephanie was unable to sit up by herself when she was a baby. Back then, I had *hope* that the pillows would help her to gain strength and stability. Now, I *knew* the pillows were simply to hold her upright.

The all too familiar fears and worries began creeping into my thoughts, but I was determined not to give in to them. I refused to believe that this was *the end* every time Stephanie leaned to the left, refused to try to stand, hesitated in her responses, stared into space, or any of the many other indicators that I knew might signal regression.

However, by late October, it was impossible to ignore the bursts of anger, the absence of spontaneous singing, and the increase in verbal aggression towards Alice, Ida, and on occasion, towards us. Still, I searched for ways to discount the reasons for her actions.

Maybe, I reasoned, she's just tired of sitting in her chair, being pushed to do exercises that she hates, and the ongoing painful needle pricks for blood tests. And, besides, she wasn't angry and aggressive *all* of the time.

But, within the next few weeks, her voice became softer, she slurred her words and, at times, she was extremely difficult to understand.

We didn't talk about what we were seeing and hearing.

I phoned Dr. Turner.

A few days later, after a thorough physical and neurological examination, Dr. Turner sat holding Stephanie's hand. "There are two possibilities to be considered. The obvious one is that there is a recurrence of the tumor. The other is the possibility that this is a delayed deterioration from the radiation therapy. Either way . . . . .it's a matter of *time.*

Recurrence. Deterioration. The words rang in my ears. Call it *recurrence*, call it *deterioration*, it still meant *terminal.* It still meant that *time* was catching up with us.

Since it was less than three weeks before Christmas, we would return after the holidays for an MRI to determine if it was the tumor causing the regression. There was no urgency to administer the test and get the results. There were no further treatments that could be given to Stephanie.

I told Robyn and Jennifer that we would be returning to the hospital for some tests after Christmas. I didn't see any need to tell them about the *recurrence* and *deterioration* until we received the results of the MRI. I knew that they knew it was serious, however, and they knew I knew that they knew. I was numb. I was drained. I wasn't ready to give the tumor new life by talking about it.

We carried on with our Christmas traditions, but there was an indiscernible melancholy that wrapped itself around my heart. I would paint a smile on my face, and I would smother the pain that hovered just beneath the surface, waiting to erupt in deep, wrenching sobs. No longer would I have to wonder if *this* Christmas was going to be the last one with all of us together.

In obvious contrast to the grandchildren's excitable and exuberant responses to their gifts, Stephanie was irritable, subdued, and disinterested. There was no anticipation in her as she ripped the paper from the gifts stacked on her wheelchair tray, no pleasure on her face when we talked to her and encouraged her to sing Christmas carols with us, no joy in her eyes as she looked at the tree and all the decorations throughout the house.

She too was drained.

We returned to the hospital for the MRI, then waited for the results. It only took a few days, but it seemed like a lifetime. I wasn't sure why it mattered . . . either result was a death sentence. But, in my mind I kept hoping that it would be *deterioration*. Maybe *deterioration* would cause slower regression in Stephanie than the tumor would. I knew that this was selfish thinking because maybe *deterioration* would give us more *time* with Stephanie, but would there be any quality to her life? Would there be more suffering?

We sat in Dr. Turner's office, and I looked at the tiles on the floor and on the ceiling, and I looked at the pictures on the wall. Nothing had changed, but I felt an urge to get up and pace across the tiles and count them . . . just to make sure. I examined the pictures. Maybe one was hanging crooked and I could straighten it.

But everything was the same.

Everything.

The pain in Dr. Turner's eyes was all the answer we needed. The tumor was active. Stephanie had three to six months to live.

We drove home in a stupor. What do you do when someone tells you that your daughter's life will be over in a matter of months? What do you do when you know there's no miracle cure waiting to rescue her one last time? What do you do when *time* is slipping away?

I had lived the last three years and three months in denial, never *truly* admitting to myself that Stephanie was gravely ill, never *truly* admitting to myself that Stephanie's tumor could *not* be vanquished, never *truly* giving up hope that, somehow, *time* would be on our side.

And when I had felt even the slightest trace of hopelessness, I had fortified myself by remembering a quote from Emily Dickinson.

> *Hope is the thing with feathers*
> *That perches in the soul,*
> *And sings the tune without the words,*
> *And never stops at all.*

I wouldn't allow myself to give up hope, despite what Dr. Turner said, despite what I was witnessing every day.

By this time, the girls understood that Stephanie's tumor was active. They were well aware of Stephanie's brief spells where she became wide-eyed, tensed her body and flexed her arms, reminiscent of the seizures that had gripped her throughout her stay at the hospital. They saw the look of either anger or terror that enveloped her face with each spell. We couldn't determine what the expression meant because she couldn't tell us.

She was no longer talking.

They were aware that she was no longer feeding herself and her appetite had declined to almost nothing, though she did continue to drink from her cup.

We returned to the hospital to have the feeding tube reinserted.

We got the suctioning machine out of the closet.

As the days and weeks wore on, Stephanie sat in her recliner, her head turned to the left, staring into space, responding to no one. We talked to her, stroked her, kissed her, held her, played her music.

By the end of February, word had spread that Stephanie had taken a turn for the worse. Family, friends and co-workers visited carrying casseroles and desserts. Hospice offered help, but we declined. Alice and Ida were reassigned, and we had new nurse's aides that appeared sporadically. I received access to the sick leave bank and stayed home with Stephanie, while Jennifer, who had graduated in December with a degree in English, took over my classes as a long-term substitute.

The rest of the world *lived* on.

As the snow melted, the crocuses appeared, the days grew longer, and the smell of farmers fertilizing their fields filtered through the doors and windows. I watched the March winds whip the branches of the Sugar Maple tree in the front yard, and felt my fear grow. How much longer could I cling to a hope that now seemed fruitless?

And when I remembered a quote by the Canadian lawyer and author, Thomas Chandler Haliburton that I often used in my English classes, my fear grew into desolation. *Hope is a pleasant acquaintance, but is an unsafe friend.*

Stephanie continued staring into space, responding to no one. We continued talking to her, stroking her, kissing her, holding her, playing her music.

By April, buds appeared on the trees and shrubs, the rain washed away the smell of the fertilized fields, and the Little Leaguers paraded through town, signaling the start of the baseball and softball season.

I searched in the bottom of Stephanie's closet and found her softball glove. It was barely worn, used mostly for show as she accompanied the team as the mascot. I visualized her wrist hanging in a downward position, as the weight of the glove caused her to fight to keep the glove on her tiny hand, but, at the same time, a smile on her face, just happy to be a part of the team.

Stephanie continued staring into space, responding to no one. We continued talking to her, stroking her, kissing her, holding her, playing her music.

As the warmth of May approached, my mind was encased with hopelessness. I wondered how our neighbors could attend to such mundane, everyday, ordinary things as planting their gardens, walking their dogs, washing their cars, while our lives were spiraling out of control, while our lives were filled with despair, while Stephanie's tumor was no longer biding *its* time, but was using up *our* time.

Desperate to hold onto memories of the good times, I gathered Special Olympic medals from her dresser drawer, held them against my cheek, rubbed my fingers over them, and closed my eyes. I saw her standing at attention with her fellow athletes, reciting the Olympic oath before the games started while we stood in the bleachers of the football field, our faces filled with pride. I remembered the look of determination on her face when she warmed up for her softball throws, her arm swinging back and forth, her fingers struggling to hold the ball firmly in the palm of her tiny hand.

Stephanie continued staring into space, responding to no one. We continued talking to her, stroking her, kissing her, holding her, playing her music.

By June my body was wrapped in a sheath of helplessness. I hadn't slept more than two hours at a time since Stephanie had had her operation; now I slept even less. And, when I did sleep, my dreams were filled with grotesque visions of an insidious, deformity that was cunningly working in the unwary, convoluted, contours of Stephanie's brain. In my dreams, I fought to free my bound arms and legs from an invisible restraint. I clawed at the barriers that I couldn't see, could only feel. I struggled to scream. I could feel my mouth moving, but there was no sound. I wanted, I needed to warn Stephanie. I needed to help her escape. I needed to safeguard my defenseless child. I needed to protect her. I needed to destroy that hideous, loathsome, evil, depraved predator. Why couldn't I stop the growth of the tumor that was spiriting away the life of our Special Angel? And always I awakened, sweating, my heart racing, knowing that I would never be able to save her.

Lydia, my favorite nurse's aide, had told me, *you're a very special person.* Special? The word rang hollowly in my head. I didn't feel very special. What was special about a mother who sat hopelessly and helplessly beside her daughter every day, unable to do anything to save her? What was special about a mother who wasn't *sure* that she could die for her children?

As the weeks passed, I moved about in a fog. My days were spent sitting on the sofa beside Stephanie in her recliner. I held her hand. I talked to her. I read to her. I played her Kenny Rogers' tapes. My nights were no longer spent on the lumpy sofa. I slept with Stephanie. I had to be near enough to make sure that nothing happened while she slept.

I couldn't shake the words that still rang in my ears from the morning after her operation. *I wanted you to sleep with me last night.*

She couldn't say those same words to me now, but I knew she would if she could.

By the middle of June her eyes closed and she slipped into a coma. I was paralyzed inside. I couldn't bear to leave her for a moment. I bathed her, changed her bed, tended to her feeding tube site, hooked her up to her feeding, moved her to her chair, suctioned her when necessary, and sat beside her holding her hand.

All day.

Every day.

As we crept into July, the heat was oppressive, setting off fierce thunder and lightning storms that rattled the windows and lit up the gray sky.

People continued to visit and I continued to acknowledge their presence, but minutes later I couldn't remember *who* came or *when* they came. I could only remember *why* they came.

I labored to keep everything looking *normal.* I smiled. I frowned. I talked. I listened. I walked. I sat. I didn't know why, I just knew I had to.

But, inside of my head it was like looking at the world through a cracked mirror—everything was distorted. I ate, but I didn't know where the food came from or whether I had cooked it. I showered and dressed, but I didn't know who provided the clean clothes. I went to bed with Stephanie at night and got up in the morning, but I didn't know who kept the bed dressed clean and made each day.

Was it morning? Was it afternoon? Was it evening? What time of day was it?

It didn't matter.

Dr. Turner continued to call, more often now. He told us that everything that was happening to Stephanie was a result of the tumor pressing on the thalamus which would eventually cause all of Stephanie's systems to shut down.

By the middle of July, her body could no longer cool itself. Her temperature shot up to 104 degrees. We purchased an air-filled rubber mattress and placed it on the bed, so I could bathe her in cool water, and we added Tylenol liquid to her feeding tube. Every day I swabbed her feverish skin, hours on end.

On the 14th, Stephanie's twenty-ninth birthday, Helen and her family came to be with us. We weren't celebrating. They were simply there for us.

As Helen and Pam watched me swab Stephanie over and over with a cloth and a pail of water, making puddles around her body on the rubber mattress, I recognized the same look in their eyes that I saw in the eyes of many of the people who visited us in the hospital. The look said, *Let her go. There's nothing more you can do.*

I said nothing, but my heart pleaded with them to understand that I *couldn't* let her go. I *couldn't* give up as long as *she* had one breath left. As long as *I* had one breath left.

But I knew they couldn't understand. She wasn't their daughter.

It was getting harder to keep Stephanie's throat clear. We were suctioning her continuously. One evening, Jennifer stood holding the machine while I put the long plastic nozzle into Stephanie's mouth, working it around the sides of her cheeks and her gums sucking up the saliva, and lately, the brown liquid, that collected endlessly.

Suddenly, Jennifer shuddered, and she screamed, "What kind of God would allow Stephanie to suffer like this? Why doesn't He just let her *die*?" She ran from the room, deep, uncontrollable sobs convulsing through her body.

Later, as I sat with my arms wrapped around Jennifer's shoulders, trying to console her, I finally admitted to myself that I had allowed my needs to overshadow the devastating grief that was engulfing the family. How self-seeking could I be, hanging onto Stephanie at all costs? How could I selfishly ignore the needs of the rest of my family? How could I be so self-absorbed with my wishes when all appreciable life was gone from Stephanie's body?

Silently, I prayed, *I give Stephanie to you, Lord. Take good care of our Special Angel.*

As the week wore on, no matter how hard I tried, I couldn't swab Stephanie's sweltering body fast enough to keep her flesh cool to the touch. She was literally burning up inside, the heat radiating through her skin, though she never perspired. At night I struggled with my need to crawl into bed with her and hold her close, but I didn't want to add my body heat to the out-of-control temperatures that were devouring her.

In the end, I did, though. How could I not?

The heat outside was threatening to reach the level of Stephanie's body temperature. The grass, lifeless and brown, crunched when it was walked on. The flowers, wasted and withered, drooped over the walls of the patio. Green, slimy algae clung to the stones around the edges of the fish pond.

As Friday evening wore on, Stephanie's temperature climbed even higher.

The air-conditioner labored uselessly.

Stephanie sat in her recliner, dressed in a pink flowered, short-sleeved pajama top and a diaper, with a white, light-weight cotton blanket thrown over her legs and feet. Despite the stifling heat that hung in the night air and the suffocating warmth that emanated from her body, her legs and feet were cold.

Sitting on the sofa next to Stephanie, holding her hand, I remembered her feet in the cold, white, sterile ICU. Frigid and lifeless. I closed my eyes, trying to dislodge the image.

Kenny Rogers' songs played softly in the background. George rested in her arm. Her tiny, crooked index finger curled around and lay on his stomach.

Heat lightning streaked silently through the sky. There was no thunder, no rain, just the splendor of white, jagged, bursts of light piercing the window panes, illuminating the room.

Stephanie was afraid of lightning. I moved closer, leaned over the arm of the sofa, and squeezed her hand. "It's okay, Stephie. Mommy's here."

She sighed deeply. Her head rolled to one side.

I looked at the maple Grandmother's clock standing against the wall between the front door and the double window . . . it chimed . . . 10 p.m.

We had just run out of *time*.

What greater pain could mortals have than this.
To see their children dead before their eyes.

Euripides

Epilogue

What do you do when your *Time* is up? What do you do when your child *passes away?* I found it difficult to use the word *died* because it sounded cold and permanent.

What do you do after you carry out what needs to be done and everyone goes home to their families, their jobs, their lives?

Look to the future? Is there a future? Of course. However, it's a different future than I ever thought I'd have. Yes, I still had my family, my job, my friends, but there was a void in my heart, my life. A part of me had *passed away.*

After the funeral, I experienced a compelling urge to get rid of Stephanie's belongings. We had buried George and some of her Special Olympics medals with her, but still her room was filled with remembrances. I began throwing away some of her clothes and packing others that were good enough to give away. I gathered dolls, stuffed animals, puzzles, toys, books and tapes, filling plastic garbage bags to be donated to a charity.

I wanted to purge myself of physical reminders of Stephanie. I told myself that I had stored memories in my heart and mind. I didn't need material things.

Then, two days later, in a frantic state of mind, I phoned Robyn and learned that she hadn't, as yet, delivered Stephanie's belongings to Goodwill. Desperately, I tore down the highway. I wasn't sure why, but I knew I wanted and needed to have Freddie, the big green frog, the last stuffed animal that Stephanie had chosen on a shopping trip to Penney's.

As urgent the need to rid the house, my life, of clothes and toys that reminded me of losing Stephanie, the need to be where Stephanie played, sang, tended George, wrote her notes, hid her treasures, and lay sleeping was even more compelling. I found myself sneaking into her room, sitting on her bed, going through her toy chest, touching the books, the remaining medals, and small stuffed animals that I had squirreled away.

I began sleeping in her bed.

I longed to dream of Stephanie, but it never happened. So anxious was I that I lay in bed at night bringing to mind times, places, happenings, visualizing her face, her crooked finger, her deep blue eyes, her skinny legs, all the time hoping that what I had once heard . . . . *the last thing you think of before you go to sleep is likely what you'll dream about*, would prove to be true for me.

Finally, after months of waiting, I did dream of Stephanie, and she appeared as she was before the seizures, before the tumor, before the devastating day after the operation.

She moved with the same slight rolling motion that defined her repaired hip bones. She wore the glasses that swallowed up the upper half of her tiny face. Her hearing aids filled and cupped her ears and stuck out from beneath her hair. Her smile was gentle and affectionate. But, as quickly as she appeared, in a dream that I no longer remembered the details, she was gone.

The next day I spent hours trying to recall the dream, trying to figure out where Stephanie fit into the dream, but in the end I didn't care. I was happy to have *seen* her.

Then, though Stephanie still appeared in my dreams, on rare occasions, I found that it wasn't enough. I wanted to touch her. I wanted to hold her. I wanted to feel her in my arms again. I lay in bed at night, concentrating on happy events, focusing on significant happenings, willing her to come into my dreams, willing her to come into my arms, willing her to fill the void in my heart.

Some of the happy events that I concentrated on were holidays. Soon, I realized that my attempt to recall holiday celebrations served two purposes. I was attempting to have Stephanie appear in my dreams so that I could hold her, but I was also making sure that I reinforced the memories that I was so desperately clinging to.

Strangely, I don't remember our first Christmas without Stephanie. I don't remember any of our first holidays without Stephanie. Did I intentionally block them from my mind? Was I sufficiently healed emotionally by then, or did I deal with them as I did most emotional situations? Did I shove the pain into the back of my mind? Did I ball my heart into a fist and not allow it to feel anything but the thud of its beat?

Did I bury my emotions with Stephanie?

As the weeks turned into months, I found myself hovering over my children and my grandchildren. I worried when they were driving, when they were at work, when they were at school, when they were socializing, when they were sick, when they weren't with *me*. I asked them to call when they left the house, when they arrived at their destination, when they returned. I continually checked on their health and well-being.

If I could lose Stephanie, couldn't I just as easily lose them, I thought?

Through all the years of Stephanie's illness, I had denied that she would die. I listened to the doctors' words, I grieved over their imparted knowledge, I labored through the day to day sorrows, but I refused to admit that I was going to lose her.

But, finally, reality set in. I did lose her. She did die.

And then the guilt began to envelop me. Would it have made a difference if I had recognized that Stephanie's headaches were more than allergies? Would it have made a difference if I had connected her weight loss to the headaches? Would it have made a difference if I had resigned from teaching and stayed home with Stephanie from the very beginning when she was diagnosed?

Did I do all that I could have done?

To help dissolve my guilt and lift my spirits, I channeled my thoughts and energies into my work. I submerged myself into the operation of my classroom. I exerted time and effort supervising extra-curricular activities. I tried to wring every bit of life out of every experience. I couldn't run away physically, but I could try to run away emotionally.

To say that I struggled with Stephanie's death would be an understatement. Surely I displayed all seven of the signs of grieving. But, at the same time, I eventually began to reconcile myself to what life was going to be like without our beloved daughter.

And though, as a family, each of us grieved in our own manner and time, we had no problem agreeing that we wanted something positive to come from Stephanie's death.

How, we wondered, could we keep Stephanie's spirit and love for life alive?

*   *   *

I stood clutching the awards certificate in my shaking hand, my speech, written on three index cards, lying on the podium in front of me. Nervously, I scanned the sea of faces in the auditorium: faculty, students, their families, their friends. I was about to share the most painful, but also cherished, details of my life. Would they understand?

Would they even care?

Briefly, I told the audience how Stephanie, a special-needs child, had died of a brain tumor. I explained that though Stephanie had been limited in her academic abilities, she knew no limitations, and she loved life. I shared how she treasured the opportunity to learn and worked hard and diligently. And, I pointed out that she had accomplished much more than any doctor ever thought she would.

I continued:

> So, we, Stephanie's family, established a scholarship in her name to help young people further their education. We determined that the student must display the qualities that we found so endearing in Stephanie. Therefore, the criteria that we have set for receiving this scholarship are as follows: The student must have a good work ethic; exhibit determination

and courage; and, most importantly, must be caring and display love for others.

And now, the first recipient of the Stephanie Ann Black scholarship is . . .

Amidst the roar of applause, I watched as the young, blond girl stood and walked to the stage, tears streaming down her cheeks. Her lower lip quivered as she accepted the certificate. She reached her arms forward and hugged me.

My eyes stung with tears, but inside of me my heart was singing. Stephanie's spirit and love for life would, indeed, live on throughout the years with each and every student that received *her* scholarship.

* * *

And now, after all these years, while the terrible pain is gone, there is still a void in our lives that nothing or no one can ever fill. But, Stephanie lives on in our hearts and in our minds. We routinely remember the *times* that Stephanie did this, said that, participated in this, competed in that, learned how to do this, learned how to do that.

Time can never take our *memories* from us.

Stephanie at 9 months

Stephanie with her sister Robyn and her father (2 yrs., 9 mos.)

Stephanie running away from home (4 yrs., 6 mos.)

Stephanie finding her Easter basket (6 yrs.)

Stephanie running the 50 yard dash. Md. State Olympics. Notice that there isn't anybody else on the track. She's last. (10 yrs.)

Stephanie with Jangles, her cat (11 yrs.)

Stephanie, with her friend Julene, receiving her medal.
Cecil County, Md. Olympics (12 yrs.)

Stephanie with Robyn and Jennifer. (16 yrs.)

Stephanie as the team Mascot. (17 yrs.)

Stephanie in her Brownie uniform. (17 yrs.)

Stephanie going to a dance with her friend, Todd. (18 yrs.)

Stephanie in her graduation gown. (21 yrs.)

Stephanie with her Gramma and
her friend, Euffie Gibson. (24 yrs.)

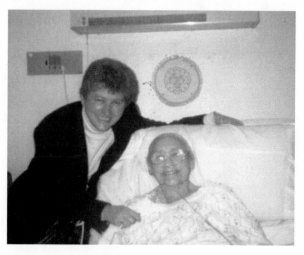

Me and Mom (May, 1990)

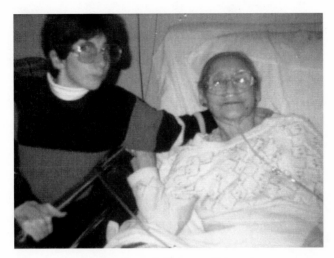

Stephanie and Gramma (24 yrs.)

Stephanie, partially bald, playing cards. (27 yrs.)

Stephanie, her mother, Robyn and Jennifer,
all wearing Stephanie's hats. (27 yrs.)

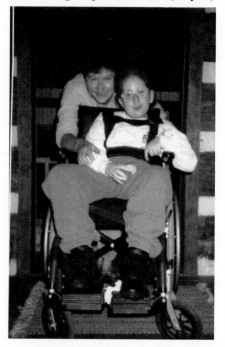

Stephanie and me (27 yrs.)

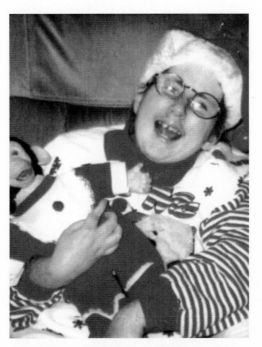

Stephanie and George (Christmas 1993)

Stephanie holding George with Elizabeth, Ronnie, Robyn, Abby,
Jennifer and Sarah (Christmas 1994)

Stephanie wrote what I always wanted to hear (28 yrs.)

ACKNOWLEDGMENTS

My immediate family has been wonderful during the time it has taken me to write this book. They have been patient, curious, and encouraging, and I thank them for that. They have not only played an important part in this book, but in all of my life. Though I chose to write this book from my perspective, I will always remember that they lived through this sad and difficult time with me. And I will always love them and be grateful for their love.

To the many parents, relatives, and friends of special-needs children and/ or children with terminal illnesses: my heart goes out to you. While there was much pain and sorrow in our lives because of Stephanie's mental and physical disabilities, and her brain tumor, there was also much happiness, joy, and excitement in our lives because of her. And so I implore you, learn to appreciate the precious uniqueness of the child with whom you've been blessed. Remember to treasure the good times, work through the bad times, and cherish the *time* you have with your *Special Angel*.

Shortly after I began writing this book, I met Maribeth Fischer, founder and president of The Rehoboth Beach Writers' Guild, and author of two books: *The Language of Goodbye* and *The Life You Longed For*. She became my mentor and friend. Her encouragement, her reminders to stay focused, and her constant pushing me to put down on paper what I did in each situation, how I reacted to each situation, helped me to go beyond the situation and tell the *real* story. And she told me many times, *keep writing your book, it matters*. Thank you so very much Maribeth.

To my sisters: Helen; Janice; and Lorraine. Thank you for reading my manuscript, making suggestions, crying and laughing with me, talking to me about your feelings, sharing your memories, and just being there for me.

To my book club members: Nan; Sandy; Judy; Marge; Susan; Maralyn; Gretchen; and Carol. Thank you for reading my manuscript, making comments, asking when I was going to do something with it, and making me laugh when I felt like I might cry.

To my school teacher friends: Sandy; Leslie; Peggy; and Marilyn. Thank you for reading my manuscript, sharing your thoughts and feelings, and encouraging me *to get it published*.

And, thank you to everyone who contributed to the development, the publishing, and distribution of this book.

Edwards Brothers, Inc.
Thorofare, NJ USA
November 22, 2011